First World War
and Army of Occupation
War Diary
France, Belgium and Germany

42 DIVISION
Divisional Troops
428 Field Company Royal Engineers
26 February 1917 - 31 March 1919

WO95/2650/2

The Naval & Military Press Ltd
www.nmarchive.com
Published in association with The National Archives

Published by

The Naval & Military Press Ltd

Unit 10 Ridgewood Industrial Park,

Uckfield, East Sussex,

TN22 5QE England

Tel: +44 (0) 1825 749494

www.naval-military-press.com

www.nmarchive.com

This diary has been reprinted in facsimile from the original. Any imperfections are inevitably reproduced and the quality may fall short of modern type and cartographic standards.

© **Crown Copyright**
Images reproduced by permission of The National Archives, London, England, 2015.

Contents

Document type	Place/Title	Date From	Date To
Heading	WO95/2650/2		
Heading	428th Field Coy R.E. Mar 1917-Mar 1919		
War Diary	Gabbari	26/02/1917	01/03/1917
War Diary	Malta	02/03/1917	05/03/1917
War Diary	Marseilles	06/03/1917	07/03/1917
War Diary	Juvisy	08/03/1917	08/03/1917
War Diary	Limeux	09/03/1917	29/03/1917
War Diary	Erondelle	30/03/1917	31/03/1917
Heading	War Diary of 428th (E.L.) Field Coy R.E. From 1st To 31st March 1917		
War Diary	Gabbari	26/02/1917	01/03/1917
War Diary	Malta	02/03/1917	05/03/1917
War Diary	Marseilles	06/03/1917	07/03/1917
War Diary	Juvisy	08/03/1917	08/03/1917
War Diary	Limeux	09/03/1917	31/03/1917
Heading	War Diary Of 428 (E Lancs) 2nd Coy RE Mar 1st To 30th April 1917		
War Diary	Erondelle	01/04/1917	05/04/1917
War Diary	Catelet	06/04/1917	30/04/1917
War Diary	War Diary Of 428 (East Lancs) Field Coy R.E. From 1st to 31st May 1917		
War Diary	Villers Faucon	01/05/1917	11/05/1917
War Diary	Ronssoy	12/05/1917	16/05/1917
War Diary	Villers Faucon	17/05/1917	18/05/1917
War Diary	Fins	19/05/1917	20/05/1917
War Diary	Metz-en Couture	21/05/1917	29/05/1917
War Diary	Havrincourt Wood	30/05/1917	31/05/1917
Heading	War Diary Of 428th (E. Lancs) Fld Coy RE From 1st to 30th June 1917		
War Diary	Havrincourt Wood	01/06/1917	15/06/1917
War Diary	No 1 Ec Ytres	15/06/1917	15/06/1917
War Diary	No 2 Ruyaulcourt	16/06/1917	16/06/1917
War Diary	No 3 Bertincourt	16/06/1917	16/06/1917
War Diary	No 4 Ruyaulcourt Coy Hdqrs	18/06/1917	19/06/1917
War Diary	Coy Hdqrs	19/06/1917	19/06/1917
War Diary	Ruyaulcourt	20/06/1917	30/06/1917
Heading	War Diary Of 428th (E.L.) Field Company R.E. From 1st to 31st July 1917		
War Diary	Mtd and No 1 Sector at Ytres No 3 Section Bertincourt HQ 2 &4 Sections Ruyaulcourt	01/07/1917	04/07/1917
War Diary	Ytres	05/07/1917	06/07/1917
War Diary	Bus HQ 2 And 4 Bihucourt No 1 And 3 Gomiecourt	06/07/1917	09/07/1917
War Diary	Bihucourt	10/07/1917	10/07/1917
War Diary	Courcelles Le-Comte	11/07/1917	31/07/1917
Heading	War Diary Of 428th (E. Lancs) Field Coy RE from 1st to 31st August 1917 (Vol 4)		
War Diary	Courcelles-Le Comte	01/08/1917	21/08/1917
War Diary	Mailly-Maillet	22/08/1917	22/08/1917
War Diary	Beaucourt Sur L'Ancre	23/08/1917	23/08/1917
War Diary	Proven	24/08/1917	24/08/1917

War Diary	Watou	25/08/1917	30/08/1917
War Diary	Ypres	31/08/1917	31/08/1917
Heading	War Diary of 428th (E.L.) Field Coy. R.E. from 1st to 30th September 1917		
War Diary	Mtd & No. 2 Section Vlamertinghe	01/09/1917	01/09/1917
War Diary	1,3 &4 Section Ypres (Ramparts)	02/09/1917	15/09/1917
War Diary	Brandhoek	16/09/1917	19/09/1917
War Diary	Winnezeele	19/09/1917	20/09/1917
War Diary	Wormhoudt	21/09/1917	21/09/1917
War Diary	Teteghem Area	22/09/1917	22/09/1917
War Diary	Le Panne	23/09/1917	23/09/1917
War Diary	Oost Dunkerque Bains	24/09/1917	30/09/1917
Heading	War Diary Of 428th (E. Lancs) Field Coy RE. From 1st to 31st October 1917		
War Diary	No 4 Section Roughtown	01/12/1917	01/12/1917
War Diary	Hdqrs Nos 1 2& 3 Sections	02/12/1917	02/12/1917
War Diary	Oost-Dunkerke Bains	03/12/1917	03/12/1917
War Diary	Mounted Section-St Idesbalde	04/12/1917	05/12/1917
War Diary	H Qrs Wulpen	06/12/1917	31/12/1917
Heading	War Diary of 428th (EL) Field Coy. RE. from 1st to 30th Nov. 1917		
War Diary	Coy. Hdqrs Wulpen No 4 Section At Div R E Dump No 1 2 & 3 Sections At Forward Billets Maison Tricar Mounted Section R Q.M. Stores Kerkepanne	01/11/1917	18/11/1917
War Diary	Wormhoudt	19/11/1917	20/11/1917
War Diary	Ebblinghem	21/11/1917	21/11/1917
War Diary	Clomenghem	22/11/1917	26/11/1917
War Diary	Robecq	27/11/1917	27/11/1917
War Diary	Essars	28/11/1917	30/11/1917
Heading	War Diary Of 428th (E.L.) Fld Coy RE From 1st To 31st December 1917		
War Diary	Essars & Le Quesnoy	01/12/1917	03/12/1917
War Diary	Le Quesnoy	04/12/1917	13/12/1917
Heading	War Diary Of 428th (East Lancs) Field Coy R.E. From 1st to 31st January 1918		
War Diary	Le Quesnoy	01/01/1918	31/01/1918
Heading	War Diary Of 428th (E. Lancs) Field Coy R.E. From 1st to 28th February 1918		
War Diary	Le Quesnoy	01/02/1918	28/02/1918
Heading	42nd Field Company R.E. March 1918		
Heading	War Diary Of 428th (E. Lancs) Fld. Coy R.E. 1st to 31st March 1918		
War Diary	Le Quesnoy	01/03/1918	22/03/1918
War Diary	Busnes	23/03/1918	23/03/1918
War Diary	Adinfer	24/03/1918	25/03/1918
War Diary	West Of Courcelles	25/03/1918	25/03/1918
War Diary	South Of Log East Wood	25/03/1918	25/03/1918
War Diary	West Of Courcelles	25/03/1918	26/03/1918
War Diary	Bucquoy	26/03/1918	26/03/1918
War Diary	Essarts	27/03/1918	29/03/1918
War Diary	Gommecourt Wood	30/03/1918	31/03/1918
Heading	428th Field Company. R.E. April 1918		
War Diary		01/04/1918	30/04/1918
Diagram etc	Advanced Dressing Station At J.15.b.5.0.		
Diagram etc	Machine Gun Dugout At J36.b.6.2.		
Diagram etc	Gas Proof Shelter For 12 Stretcher Cases		

War Diary		01/05/1918	31/05/1918
War Diary	Pas	01/06/1918	07/06/1918
War Diary	Bus	08/06/1918	30/06/1918
War Diary	Sheet 57.D. Coy H.Q.& No. 1 To 4 Section at Bus-Les Artois (J.20.b.5.0) tspt lenis at J 31.b.2.8 (on Bus-Louvencourt Road)	01/07/1918	31/07/1918
War Diary	Coy. H.Q. 9 Nos. 1 To 4 Section At J 2a.b.5.0. (Bus As.artois Woods) Mtd Section & Transport J 31.b.2.8. on Bus-Louvencourt Rd) Sheet 57c & 57d	01/08/1918	13/08/1918
Heading	Machine Gun Emplacement No.2 at J.30b.7.6 No 1 and at J.30.d.7.6 Observation Post		
Diagram etc	Machine Gun Emplacement No 1 And Observation Post At J.30.b.7.6. Sheet 57d.		
Diagram etc	Machine Gun Emplacement No 2 At J30b76 Sheet 57d		
Diagram etc	Machine Gun Emplacement No 1 And Observation Post At J.30.b.7.6. Sheet 57d		
War Diary		01/09/1918	29/09/1918
War Diary	Coy H Q & Diamounted Camp P12.b.5.0 (Havrincourt Wood) Transport Lines Bertincourt	01/10/1918	31/10/1918
War Diary	Jeune Bois	01/11/1918	04/11/1918
War Diary	Solesmes	05/11/1918	05/11/1918
War Diary	Le Quesnoy	06/11/1918	06/11/1918
War Diary	Le Cornoy	07/11/1918	07/11/1918
War Diary	La Corne	08/11/1918	08/11/1918
War Diary	Various	09/11/1918	09/11/1918
War Diary	Hautmont	10/11/1918	30/11/1918
Heading	War Diary 428th (E. Lancs) Field Coy R.E. From 1st to 31st December 1918		
War Diary	Hautmont	01/12/1918	14/12/1918
War Diary	Lameries	15/12/1918	15/12/1918
War Diary	Binche	16/12/1918	16/12/1918
War Diary	Fontaine L'Eveque	17/12/1918	18/12/1918
War Diary	Charleroi	19/12/1918	31/12/1918
War Diary		07/12/1918	13/12/1918
Heading	War Diary Of 428th (E. Lancs) Field Coy RE From Jan 1st to 31st 1919 (Volume 6)		
War Diary	Charleroi	01/01/1919	31/03/1919

WO 95
2650/2

42ND DIVISION

428TH FIELD COY R.E.

MAR 1917 - MAR 1919.

(FRANCE)

Army Form C. 2118.

WAR DIARY
or
INTELLIGENCE SUMMARY.
(Erase heading not required.)

Instructions regarding War Diaries and Intelligence Summaries are contained in F.S. Regs., Part II and the Staff Manual respectively. Title pages will be prepared in manuscript.

428¢ (E. LANCS) FIELD COY. R.E.

MARCH 1917

Hour, Date, Place	Summary of Events and Information	Remarks and references to Appendices
GABBARI 26-2-1917	Remainder of Coy (3 Officers & 130 O.R.) marched from Gabbari Alexandria to docks and embarked on HMS HUNTSPILL for Salonica.	
27-2-1917	Sailed from Alexandria harbour 0930	
28-2-1917	} at sea.	
1-3-17		
MALTA 2-3-17	At sea. Arrived @ MALTA D 2300 and anchored in the harbour.	
3-3-17	Left MALTA 1000 and proceeded manoeuvre	
4-3-17	} at sea.	
5-3-17		
MARSEILLES 6-3-17	Arrived at MARSEILLES. 0600. Disembarked 1430 and marched to public and entrained at 1500 at MARSEILLES. 1530.	
7-3-17	Passed through various places including LYONS, DIJON &1.	
JUVISY 8-3-17	Arrived JUVISY 0230. A halt of 2 hours was made and general entrainment at 1030 passed through CREIL, AMIENS. Detrained at PONT-REMY. 2200 marched to LIMEUX to the billets	
LIMEUX 9-3-17	arriving there at 0230 in the morning & other ranks had breakfast at Alexandria carriages on 23rd Feby. Except the Coy and billets were arranged and 2 Blanket issued to O/R, kit 2 was served out	
10-3-17	Bn. in Hospital at MARSEILLES. 1 horse had died of exposure during journey return on trolls from QMS Rifles & Bayonets, billets were cleaned up. Ammn D PONT REMY 61 horse were drawn from Divisional Horse Transport Depot ABBEVILLE	
11-3-17	Church parade. Drawing of kits completed today. Few men engaged on special employ and the RSM was attached with this Coy. & inspected from NCOs and the men in their various to known. In respects was attached from Friday next Officers to go about for instruction	

(73989) W4141—463. 400,000. 9/14. H.&J.Ltd. Forms/C. 2118/10.

WAR DIARY or INTELLIGENCE SUMMARY

Army Form C. 2118.

Places	Date	Hour	Summary of Events and Information	Remarks and references to Appendices
LIMEUX	12.3.17		Class of J.N.C.Os and nights under R.S.M. Lowery. No. 1 & 4 section parties and motor drill. No. 2 section preparing to move. No. 3 on special employment. Athletics trenches. Fire Buckets. P.R.	
	13.3.17		Class as on 12th. No. 1 & 2 section as on 12th. No. 3 again on special duties. No. 2 section moved to CHAVRS (2 miles NE of ABBEVILLE) and GRAND LAVIERS.	
	14.3.17		Class under R.S.M. as on 13th. Coy occupied in Revts Work in morning & duties in the afternoon. Specially employed parties skeleton trenches at HUPPY returning & HALLENCOURT. Various bodies at HUPPY experimenting with borings etc & seen for timings taken & reports to.	
	15.3.17		The Coy (less specially employed and No. 2 section) were exercised in Revts Work in the morning and various same given by section commanders in the afternoon. Specially employed in skeleton trenches C.I. through refugees detainments at HALLENCOURT. to work for 429 & Field Coy and 1 for R.E. H.Q. were drawn from Permit Depot @ ABBEVILLE.	
	16.3.17		No. 1 & 4 Sections were employed on Revts Work, loading & Unloading & Relocating Construction Bridge. N.C.Os Class under R.S.M. Lowery. No. 2 Section & specially employed as on 15th. 4 N.C.Os were sent to 429 Fld Coy R.E. at CORBIE by Road Lorries L Lanlined 429 Coy on being left in the charge of 426 Fld Coy sick. The three for R.E. H.Q. was attached to 428 Fld Coy for use by the R.S.M.	
	17.3.17		No. 2 section were specially employed as on 16th. N.C.Os Class under R.S.M. Lowery also lessons on 4 duty was addressed to 2nd Stationary hospital ABBEVILLE by march. 1000 where they had baths and then clothes fumigated.	
	18.3.17		Specially employed as 1. No. 2 section as on 17. rehearsals party under the Coy on fatigue. Sofia Scam for front time Marched to 28 Feb to R.E. for unloading of purposes.	

WAR DIARY or INTELLIGENCE SUMMARY

Army Form C. 2118.

Place	Date	Hour	Summary of Events and Information	Remarks and references to Appendices
Entrained LIMEUX	18-3-17		6.C. Coy with 3 N.C.Os & Batman left Coy to be attached to 1st Div. for course of instruction in front line trenches. 9.O.R. left Central Infantry School FLEXICOURT for 4 short course on the instruction of rapid wire entanglements. No.1 section went with transport proceeded by road to FLEXICOURT for work on hutting at 4th Army Infantry School.	
	19.3.17		The Coy. less No. 1 & 2 Sections sent the men specially employed on obstetion benches, mitre & stencils etc. were engaged on trainers field coy. and 4 Engineers during the morning and had a lecture on Tools & Demolition formulas and the Knuckleduster on trench warfare in the afternoon under the R.S.M.	
	20.3.17		The Coy. less No.1 & 2 sections - specially employed were inspected in a route march from CROUY about 1700 bridging formed as 1 officer and 26 O.R. of No.2 Section rejoined their the afternoon on Friday to PONT REMY bridging in with their section transport. No.0.R. were left to complete the work at GRAND LAVIERS.	
	21.3.17		The Coy. less No.1 Section and specially employed were employed during the morning in physical drill, musketry and a lecture on trench experience by Lieut J.P. Schlin. Coy. Signallers were trained in signalling and map reading and a wire class [?] instruction in trench was commenced under the interpreter. In the afternoon the Coy were paid and were given a lecture on the construction of square trestles. 2 officers and 5 Offr. & 16 O.R. left taken by No.2 Section rejoined the Coy. and the party from the Central Infantry School also rejoined.	
	22.3.17		Signallers & Trench Class were carried on as on 21st and the remainder of the Coy. less specially employed were engaged in the formation of square trestle trestles and the construction of Rapid Barbed Wire/ entanglements with some further practice in the construction	

Army Form C. 2118.

WAR DIARY
or
INTELLIGENCE SUMMARY.
(Erase heading not required.)

Place	Date	Hour	Summary of Events and Information	Remarks and references to Appendices
LIMEUX	23.3.17		The C.O. & all N.C.O. Sections 1 were given a lecture on Preventive measures by the C.O. & no N.C.O. on the first parade after which the C.O. less specially employed were occupied in training from 23rd inst. A further lecture on Gas was given in the afternoon.	
	24.3.17		During the morning the C.O. was engaged in Physical Training and a further lecture on Gas, Rapid wiring and trestle bridging was also carried on. A party proceeded to 726 Coy Baths at HUPPY during the afternoon for bath. Remainder as on 23rd.	
	25.3.17		A party of Sappers were given instruction in Rapid wiring during the morning. Remainder the Coy visited D26 Bee Baths at HUPPY. 2Lt KENNARD & 17 O.R. were attacked by 1/10 Man. and a party of 4 N.C.O. 1/9 Man. and 1/5 E.Lancs to instruct the infantry in rapid wiring. Church Parade was held in the evening.	
	26.3.17		Capt Curtis & 2Lt Entwistle 1st Echelon H.Q. proceeded to ERONDELLE with N.C.O. 3 & 4 Sections for training in Pontooning & floating bridges. Joiners occupied in completing work intended at NIMEUX.	
	27.3.17		Bridging training was carried on at ERONDELLE and instruction in barbed wire defences with 126 Batt. at HUPPY. Joiners at LIMEUX as on 26.	
	28.3.17		As on 27.	

Army Form C. 2118.

WAR DIARY
or
INTELLIGENCE SUMMARY.
(Erase heading not required.)

Place	Date	Hour	Summary of Events and Information	Remarks and references to Appendices
LIMEUX	29.3.17.		Detachment at ERONDELLE and HUPPY with 126 Bde. Carried mas in 28'. Roign Remaneder J. Cy. less not Sections, who are still at Central Infantry School, FLIXECOURT, moved from LIMEUX to ERONDELLE.	
ERONDELLE	30.3.17.		Bridging practice at ERONDELLE continues. Former engage in advanced training from D.H.Q. Detachment attached to 126 Bde. providing men down to MERCOURT and PONT REMY billetting area.	
	31.3.17.		Cy. engages as on 30'.	

(sd) J.G.REDDICK Major
OC/51stFd.Cy.R.E.

Apr. 1st 1917.

CONFIDENTIAL

WAR DIARY
of
428th (E.L.) Field Coy. R.E.

from 1st to 31st March. 1917

(Volume 4)

Vol 17 2

Army Form C. 2118.

WAR DIARY
or
INTELLIGENCE SUMMARY.
(Erase heading not required.)

ORIGINAL

Instructions regarding War Diaries and Intelligence Summaries are contained in F. S. Regs., Part II. and the Staff Manual respectively. Title pages will be prepared in manuscript.

428th (E. Lancs.) Field Coy. R.E.

Place	Date	Hour	Summary of Events and Information	Remarks and references to Appendices
GABBARI.	26th Feby.	---	Remainder of Company (3 officers + 120 other ranks) marched from Gabbari, Alexandria to docks and embarked on H.M.T. "Huntspill" for overseas.	A.Q.
	27"	---	Sailed from Alexandria harbour @ 0930.	A.Q.
	28"	---	at Sea.	A.Q.
	1" March	---		A.Q.
MALTA.	2"	---	at sea. Arrived @ MALTA 2300 and anchored in the harbour.	A.Q.
	3"	---	left MALTA 1000 and proceeded overseas.	A.Q.
	4"	---	at Sea.	A.Q.
	5"	---		A.Q.
MARSEILLES.	6	---	arrived MARSEILLES 0600. Disembarked @ 1430 and marched to sidings and entrained @ 1500. Left Marseilles 1530.	A.Q.
	7"	---	Passed through various places, including LYONS, DIJON &c.	A.Q.
JUVISY.	8"	---	Arrived JUVISY 0230. A halt of 8 hours was made and the journey continues @ 1030. A.Q. Passed through CREIL, AMIENS. Detrained @ PONT REMY 2200. Marched to LIMEUX	A.Q.

1577 Wt.W10791/1773 500,000 1/15 D. D. & L. A.D.S.S./Forms/C. 2118.

Army Form C. 2118.

WAR DIARY
or
INTELLIGENCE SUMMARY.
(Erase heading not required.)

Instructions regarding War Diaries and Intelligence Summaries are contained in F.S. Regs., Part II. and the Staff Manual respectively. Title pages will be prepared in manuscript.

Place	Date	Hour	Summary of Events and Information	Remarks and references to Appendices
LIMEUX	8th March	---	to the billets arranged.	Jr. G
	9th	---	arriving here @ 0230 this morning. Other ranks who had embarked @ Alexandria on 22nd Feb. and 2 officers, 88 other ranks and * horses who had embarked @ Alexandria on 23rd Feb. rejoined the Company and billets were re-arranged and 2nd blankets issued. * 1 O.R. has gone to hospital @ MARSEILLES. # 1 horse had died @ Sea.	Jr. G
	10th	---	Sections began rationing independently, drawing rations in bulk from C.Q.M.S. Rifles + Bayonets were drawn @ PONT REMY. 61 horses were drawn from Advanced Horse Transport Depot, ABBEVILLE.	Jr. G
	11th	---	Church Parade. Drawing of rifles tc. completed today. Few men engaged on special employment. The R.S.M. was attached to this Company to instruct the junior N.C.Os and a few men in a special course of training tc. An interpreter was attached from today. Lt/Cpl Clayton to Gas School for instruction.	Jr. G
	12th	---	Class of 30 N.C.Os and Sappers under R.S.M. Sowray. No 1 & 4 Sections, Pontoon + Trestle drill. No 2 Section preparing to move. No 3 on special employment. (Latrines, benches, his buckets, etc)	Jr. G
	13th	---	Class as on 12th No 1 + 4 Section as on 12th. No 3 again on special duties. No 2 Sec.	Jr. G

WAR DIARY
or
INTELLIGENCE SUMMARY.
(Erase heading not required.)

Army Form C. 2118.

Place	Date	Hour	Summary of Events and Information	Remarks and references to Appendices
LIMEUX.	13th	(cont)	No 2 Section moved to CAOURS (2 miles N.E. of ABBEVILLE,) and GRAND LAVIERS taking Section Transport.	L.O.
	14th March		Class under R.S.M. as on 13th. Company exercised in Route March in morning + lectures in the afternoon. Specially employed, fixing Ablution benches @ HUPPY, repairing latrines @ HALLENCOURT, repairing boiler @ HUPPY, experimenting with corrugated iron for troughs, making signboards.	L.O. L.O.
	15th	--	The Company, (less Specially employed and No 2 Section) were exercised in a route march in the morning and lectures were given by Section Commanders in the afternoon. Specially employed on ablution benches. C.I. troughs, repairing latrines seats at HALLENCOURT. Ten horses for 429th Field Coy. and 1 for R.E. Hdqrs. were drawn from Remount Depot @ ABBEVILLE.	L.O.
	16th	--	Nos 1 + 4 Sections were employed on Welbar Trestle. Bridge + C.O.'s class under R.S.M. Soway, No 2 Section + Specially employed as on 15th. 9 Horses were sent to 429th Fd Co R.E. at CORBIE. by road.) under 2/Lt Eastwood 429th Fd Co, one being left on the charge of 428th Fd Co Sick. The horse for R.E. Hqrs was attached to 426th Fd Co for use by R.S.M.	L.O. L.O. L.O.

Army Form C. 2118.

WAR DIARY
or
INTELLIGENCE SUMMARY.
(Erase heading not required.)

Instructions regarding War Diaries and Intelligence Summaries are contained in F. S. Regs., Part II and the Staff Manual respectively. Title pages will be prepared in manuscript.

Place	Date	Hour	Summary of Events and Information	Remarks and references to Appendices
LIMEUX.	17th		No 2 Section and specially employed as on 16th. N.C.O's class under RSM Soway also carried on. A party was sent to 2nd Stationary Hospital ABBEVILLE by march route where they had baths and their clothing etc fumigated.	R.A.
	18th		Specially employed and No 2 Section as on 17th. Advanced party who left Coy in Egypt reported after being in front line attached to 23rd F.O Co R.E. for instructional purposes. O.C. Coy with 3 N.C.O.'s & batman left Coy to be attached to 1st Div for course of instruction in front line trenches. 9 O.R. left for Central Infantry School FLEXICOURT for a short course on the construction of "Rapid" wire entanglements. No 1 Section with all transport proceeded by road to FLEXICOURT for work on putting at 4th Army Infantry School.	J.G.
	19th		The Coy, less Nos 1 & 2 Sections and the men specially employed on addition trenches, making stencils etc, were engaged on training both Infantry and Engineer during the morning, and had a lecture on Timber & Demolition Formulas, and the Pamphlet on Trench Warfare in the afternoon under the R.S.M.	J.G.

WAR DIARY
or
INTELLIGENCE SUMMARY.
(Erase heading not required.)

Army Form C. 2118.

Place	Date	Hour	Summary of Events and Information	Remarks and references to Appendices
LIMEUX.	20th		The Coy less No's 1 & 2 Sections & specially employed were exercised in a route march during the morning to PONT REMY and back, and were given lectures during the afternoon on bridging formulas. 1 Officer & 26 O.R. of the 2 Sect rejoined coy on the evening from CAOURS. about 1700 bringing in with them the Section transport. 16 o.r. were left to complete the work at GRAND LAVIERS.	J.R.
	21st		The Coy less No 1 Sect and specially employed were engaged during the morning on physical drill, musketry, & a lecture on trench experience by Lt Col J.P. Echlin. Coy Signallers were trained in signalling and map reading, and a small class for instruction in French was commenced under the Interpreter. In the afternoon the coy were paid and were given a lecture on the construction of square timber trestles. 8 of the 16 o.r. left behind by No 2 Section rejoined the Coy, and the party from the Central Infantry School also rejoined.	J.R.
	22nd		Signallers and French classes were carried on as on 21st, and the remainder of the Coy less specially employed were occupied on the formation of square timber trestles and the construction of bridge with same, also on practice	J.R.

Army Form C. 2118.

WAR DIARY
or
INTELLIGENCE SUMMARY.
(Erase heading not required.)

Instructions regarding War Diaries and Intelligence Summaries are contained in F. S. Regs., Part II. and the Staff Manual respectively. Title pages will be prepared in manuscript.

Place	Date	Hour	Summary of Events and Information	Remarks and references to Appendices
LIMEUX.	22nd (cont'd)		in the construction of Rapid Barbed Wire entanglement.	J.R.
	23rd.		The Coy less No 1 Section were given a lecture on Gas and Revolver fire measures by the Coy Gas N.C.O. on the first parade, after which the Coy less specially employed were occupied at training as on 22nd. A further lecture on Gas was given in the afternoon.	J.R.
	24th.		During the morning the Coy was engaged on Physical Training and a further lecture on Gas. Rapid wiring and trestle bridging was also carried on. A party proceeded to 126 Bde Baths at Huppy during the afternoon for a bath. Remainder employed as on 23rd.	J.R.
	25th.		A party of sappers were given instruction in Rapid wiring during the morning. The remainder of the Coy visited the 126 Bde Baths at Huppy. 2 Lt Kennard and 14 OR were attached to 1/10 Man and a party of 1 OR to 1/9th Man and 1/5th Lancs to instruct the infantry in Rapid wiring. Church parade was held in the evening.	J.R.
	26th.		Capt Counsell & 2Lts Epworth & Echlin J.P. proceeded to ERONDELLE with Nos 3 and 4 Sections for training on pontooning and floating bridges. Joiners occupied completing work on hand at LIMEUX.	J.R.
	27th.		Bridging training was carried on at ERONDELLE and instruction in Barbed wire defences with 126 Bde at HUPPY. Joiners at LIMEUX as on 26th.	J.R.

Army Form C. 2118.

WAR DIARY
or
INTELLIGENCE SUMMARY.
(Erase heading not required.)

Place	Date	Hour	Summary of Events and Information	Remarks and references to Appendices
LIMEUX	28th 29th		As on 27th. Detachment at ERONDELLE and HUPPY etc. will 126 Bde carried on as on 28th.	
	30th		Adopts and remainder of coy, less No 1 Section who are still at Central Infantry School FLEXICOURT, moved from LIMEUX to ERONDELLE. Bridging practice at ERONDELLE continued. Former engaged on notice boards for D.H.Q. Detachment attached to 126 Bde to work, moved down to LIERCOURT and PONT REMY billeting area.	J.R. J.Q. J.Q.
	31st		Coy engaged as on 30th.	

In the field
April 1st 1919

J. Riddick
Major
OC 428 (2 Ts) Co
(2 Roma) R.E.

Confidential

WO 3

WAR DIARY

of

428 (E.Lancs) Fd Co. RE

from 1st to 30th April 1917.

(Volume 4)

Army Form C. 2118.

WAR DIARY

INTELLIGENCE SUMMARY.

(Erase heading not required.)

ORIGINAL

428th (East Lancs) Field Company. R.E.

Place	Date	Hour	Summary of Events and Information	Remarks and references to Appendices
ERONDELLE	1/7/17		Church Parade in morning. Coy. had afternoon off duty.	
do.	2/7/17		Dismantling bridges, etc.	
do.	3/7/17		Dismantling bridges, and preparing to move.	
do.	4/7/17		Coy. (less No.1. Section at FLIXIECOURT) marched from ERONDELLE to PONT REMY Station and moved by rail to CHUIGNES marching from there through DOMPIERRE to BECQUINCOURT, and bivouaced for the night.	
	5/7/17		Moved by march route from BECQUINCOURT to LE CATELET, via BIACHES, PERONNE and DOINGT.	
CATELET.	6/7/17		Sections engaged on various kinds of work, clearing ground for new 3rd Corps H.Q. Tents were drawn from D.A.D.O.S. 59th Division. There were pitched, and Coy. moved from their billets to the tents. No.3 Section on clearing camping ground, etc. Nos. 2 & 4 Sections employed on erection of "Nissen" Huts in Camp A.	
do.	7/7/17		All 3 Sections engaged on hutting, etc.	
do.	8/7/17		As on 6th.	
do.	9/7/17		As on 9th. II Lieut. Saint and No.1 Section rejoined Coy. from FLIXIECOURT.	
do.	10/7/17		The Coy. (including No.1 Section) on "Nissen" Huts. 2 Sections of 427th Field Coy. R.E. and 125th Bde. Pioneers reported for work with 428th Coy. In the afternoon Coy. moved over to BIAS WOOD. 100 Pioneers from 126 Bde. reported for work, instruction etc. 1 Officer and 27 O.R. No.3 Reinforcement Coy. R.E. and 3 R.A.M.C. report for works on Corps. H.Q. and are to be rationed by 428th Coy. R.E.	
do.	11/7/17			

WAR DIARY

INTELLIGENCE SUMMARY.

(Erase heading not required.)

Army Form C. 2118.

ORIGINAL

Place	Date	Hour	Summary of Events and Information	Remarks and references to Appendices
CATELET	12/7/17		The Coy. (less specially employed) and all attached, engaged on "Nissen" Huts, and Hospital Huts in Camps A and B.	
do.	13/7/17		As on 12th.	
do.	14/7/17		As on 13th.	
do.	15/7/17		Party of 1 N.C.O. and 5 Sappers rejoined Coy. from work on Divl. Bombing School at MERICOURT-SUR-SOMME.	
do.	16/7/17		The whole Coy. engaged on hutting as above.	
do.	17/7/17		As on 16th. Rapid wiring Parties returned from 1/9th & 1/10th M/c & 1/5th East Lancs.	
do.	18/7/17		As on 17th. No. 4 Section commenced erection of "Adrian" Huts on Site "D" (BIAS WOOD)	
do.	19/7/17		As on 18th.	
do.	20/7/17		As on 19th. No. 4 Section at CARTIGNY on huts for French Mission	
do.	21/7/17		No. 1 Section commence 4 days Special course of training. Nos. 2 & 3 Sections on A, B, & C. Camps, Garage, and Crater at Cross Roads at Catelet.	
do.	22/7/17		No. 4 Section as on 20th. Nos. 1 and 3 Sections have baths. No. 4 as on 21st. No. 2 on A.B.C. Camps, Garage, and Crater at Cross Roads at Catelet.	
do.	23/7/17		No. 1 Section continue training. No. 4 as on 22nd. No. 3. take over work from No. 2 on Corps Headquarters etc. No. 2 have baths.	
do.	24/7/17		No. 1 as on 23rd. No. 2 take over from No. 4, who have baths. No. 3 as on 23rd.	
do.	25/7/17		Nos. 1 and 3 Sections as on 24th. No. 4 Section resume work on French Mission No. 2 on Crater at Catelet Cartigny, and erection of "Adrian" Huts in BIAS WOOD	
do.	26/7/17		No. 1 take over from No. 2, who go on training. Nos. 3 & 4 as on 25th.	

ORIGINAL
Army Form C. 2118.

WAR DIARY
~~INTELLIGENCE~~ SUMMARY.
(Erase heading not required.)

Instructions regarding War Diaries and Intelligence Summaries are contained in F.S. Regs., Part II and the Staff Manual respectively. Title pages will be prepared in manuscript.

Place	Date	Hour	Summary of Events and Information	Remarks and references to Appendices
CATELET.	27/7		Nos 1, 3 & 4 Sections as on 26th. No. 2. Section training reserve work on erection of "Adrian" Huts in BIAS WOOD. Corpl. Cliffe and 12 others were attached to C.R.E. Personnel for work on town improvements.	Web App B App C App D App E
do	28/7		As on 27th.	
do	29/7		Party employed dismantling tarpaulin shacks in camp preparatory to move. Corpl. Cliffe and party rejoined Coy from C.R.E's. The whole Company with pioneers	
do	30/7		moved by march route to VILLERS FAUCON and bivouacked for the night.	

K.H.M.S.
Capt,
for major,
O.C. 416th (E. Lancs) Field Coy RE

Vol 4

WAR DIARY

of

428 (East Lancs) Field Coy. R.E.

from 1st to 31st May. 1917

(Volume 4)

Original

WAR DIARY
or
INTELLIGENCE SUMMARY.
(Erase heading not required.)

Army Form C. 2118.

Place	Date	Hour	Summary of Events and Information	Remarks and references to Appendices
VILLERS FAUCON	1st May/17.		428th (E Lancs) Field Company R.E.	
			During the morning the Company moved from Roadside Bivouac (ST EMILIE – ROISEL ROAD) to the new bivouac at 62c.E19.b.18. At night the Company were employed on wiring in front of firing line from 62c F11.d89 to F18.c08.	A.N.
		2ᵐ	Company engaged on night work as on 1st.	
		3ᵈ	As on 2ⁿᵈ.	
		4ᵗʰ	No. 2 & 3 Sections moved to new billets in village of RONSSOY. The Company was engaged @ night as on the 3ʳᵈ plus additional wiring from F11.d37 to F11.d98. Constructing Machine Gun posts at F12.c05 and Lewis Gun posts at F11.d82. The Communication trench was commenced from F11.d69 to F11.d97.	
		5ᵗʰ	As on 4ᵗʰ.	
		6ᵗʰ	As on 5ᵗʰ with the addition of strong posts at F17.b63 and F11.d98.	
		7ᵗʰ	As on 6ᵗʰ with the addition of widening C.T. to GUILLEMONT FARM from F18.c2/ strong posts at F11.b36.	
		8ᵗʰ	As on 7ᵗʰ.	
		9ᵗʰ	As on 8ᵗʰ. Machine gun position at F17.b63 and intermediate trench from F11.b36 to F11.d98. A sap was commenced in the GUILLEMONT FARM trench to Northern bombing post.	

WAR DIARY or INTELLIGENCE SUMMARY

Army Form C. 2118.

Place	Date	Hour	Summary of Events and Information	Remarks and references to Appendices
VILLERS FAUCON	10th May/17		As on 9th with the addition of commencement of second sap, in GILLEMONT FARM trenches to Southern bombing post.	O.R.
	11th		As on 10th.	
RONSSOY.	12th		As on 11th. Southern sap completed - average depth 2'. Nos 1 & 4 Sections 1 Company Headquarters moved to billets in RONSSOY. The Mounted Section with horses and Transport remaining at VILLERS FAUCON. The Company took over right sub sector from 427 Field Coy R.E. from F.18.c.08 to F.29.a.85. A party was engaged wiring on the wire front at night.	O.R.
	13th		Company engaged in wiring at night from F.13.b.27 to F.13.6.69. Communicating trenches were commenced from F.11.630 to F.11.a.50 and F.11.a.97 to F.11.c.74. The Southern Sap from GILLEMONT FARM trench was deepened to 3'.	O.R.
	14th		As on 13th plus wiring F.29.a.85 to F.24.a.60.	O.R.
	15th		As on 14th plus wiring at GILLEMONT FARM.	O.R.
	16th		As on 15th.	O.R.
	17th		Company hands over work and billets in RONSSOY to Field Squadron, 2d Cavalry Bde. Company at 9.30 p.m. to billets vacated by 427 Fd Coy R.E. near VILLERS FAUCON @ 9.00.	O.R.
VILLERS FAUCON	18th		Company engaged in preparing to move and training.	O.R.
FINS.	19th		Company moved from VILLERS FAUCON @ 5.30 am. by march route to FINS. Sleeping three to the night	O.R.

Army Form C. 2118.

WAR DIARY
or
INTELLIGENCE SUMMARY.
(Erase heading not required.)

Instructions regarding War Diaries and Intelligence Summaries are contained in F. S. Regs., Part II. and the Staff Manual respectively. Title pages will be prepared in manuscript.

Place	Date	Hour	Summary of Events and Information	Remarks and references to Appendices
FINS.	20 May/17		The Company, less, Mounted Section and Transport, moved from FINS @ 8.30pm, marching to METZ-en-COUTURE.	Q.R.
METZ-en-COUTURE	21st.		Took over @ 6pm from 96 Field Coy RE: Headquarters at 57c-Q.19.d.99. Billets in METZ and section of front line defences. At night No. 1 & 3 Sections engaged in spitlockers near front line stretches. No. 2 on well and roads at TRESCAULT. No.4 on roads and water supply in METZ, and on Reserve Line.	Q.R.
	22d		As on 21st.	Q.R.
	23d		As on 22d. R.E. Dump established at Q.19.d.99.	Q.R.
	24th		New camp site selected at 57c - P.18.c.77. and work on the erection of bivouacs commenced. Reserve Line fire trench marked out from Q.11.a.43 to Q.12.c.87. Construction of a bridge over CT at Q.10.d.99.	R.R. Q.R.
	25th		Parties of 9 R.E.'s were attached to the Battalion in line, and work on Batt. Hdqrs. and shelters in the trenches was commenced. Work on new camp site continues.	Q.R.
	26th		As on 25th. TRESCAULT was searched for mines etc. Charges were removed from 3 houses in the village and from under a culvert at Q.4.c.57.	Q.R.
	27th		As on 26th. New R.E. Dump established @ P.18.C.52., and materials from existing Dump transferred.	Q.R.
	28th		Reconnaissance made for trench tramway from DECAUVILLE terminus (TRESCAULT. A hand power Hadlica pump set to work at TRESCAULT WELL and storage tanks were made. Hose from HAVRINCOURT WOOD	Q.R.

Army Form C. 2118.

WAR DIARY
or
INTELLIGENCE SUMMARY.
(Erase heading not required.)

Instructions regarding War Diaries and Intelligence Summaries are contained in F. S. Regs., Part II. and the Staff Manual respectively. Title pages will be prepared in manuscript.

Place	Date	Hour	Summary of Events and Information	Remarks and references to Appendices
METZ-en-Couture	29th May/17	As on 28th		G.R
	30th		Handed over section of front to 470th Field Coy R.E., 59 Division, also Headquarters and billets in METZ. The Company moved to new camp site in HAVRINCOURT WOOD. Reserve line marked out ready for infantry working parties to dig & further G.R. Reconnaissance was made for Trench Tramway to TRESCAULT.	
HAVRINCOURT WOOD.	31st		Company engaged on work on new headquarters for battalions and improving Z.O Company's new camp.	

J.C Riddich
MAJOR.
O.C. 428th E.L. Fd. Co. R.E.

428TH
(EAST LANCS.)
FIELD COMPANY, R.E.
No. ....
Date 31/5/17

Vol 5

ORIGINAL

Confidential

WAR DIARY

of

428th (E. Lancs) Fd. Co. R.E.

June 1st to 30th June 1917.

(Volume 4)

WAR DIARY or INTELLIGENCE SUMMARY

Army Form C. 2118.

428th (E. Lancs) Fd. Coy. R.E.

Place	Date	Hour	Summary of Events and Information	Remarks and references to Appendices
HAVRINCOURT WOOD	June 1st		Company employed on splinter proof shelters (Q4 a 7.1. to Q12 b 16). 3/ in all — 27 of these were afterwards handed over to 59th Division. (Q5 c 47 to Q12 b 16). Covered approaches to Right and left Btn. forward dumps carried on with. In preparation for new advanced front line communication trenches to forward T heads were tapes out and T heads wired in. TRESCAULT water supply Q10 a 45.65. carried on with work on pump and engine house - preparations for tanks of 2000 gallons storage capacity.	J.R.
	2nd		As on 1st. Covers for tanks and flumes to same at Q10 a 45.65 completed.	J.R.
	3rd		As on 2nd. Further lengths of C.T.s marked out from A Sap to E Sap. Carried on with water supply at TRESCAULT. Covered approaches to Right and left Btn. forward dumps completed.	J.R.
	4th		As on 3rd. Carried on with work on new saps and water supply at Q10 a 45.65. Commenced fitting up Battalion Hdqrs. Dugouts at Q10 a 44 and Q3 c 84 - Cleared tree trunks &c from new saps D + E. Fixed loose rails at METZ BREWERY.	J.R.
	5th		As on 4th. Reconnaissance of route for Trench Tramway to TRESCAULT main.	J.R.
	6th		Men had ½ day's holiday after Church Parade.	J.R.
	7th		As on 6th. Commenced taping out fire trays to form connecting fire trench between Saps ABCD + E. Clearing obstacles and tree trunks in Sap E and in front. Erecting camouflage at TRESCAULT crossroads.	J.R.

WAR DIARY
INTELLIGENCE SUMMARY

Army Form C. 2118.

(Erase heading not required.)

Instructions regarding War Diaries and Intelligence Summaries are contained in F. S. Regs., Part II. and the Staff Manual respectively. Title pages will be prepared in manuscript.

Place	Date	Hour	Summary of Events and Information	Remarks and references to Appendices
HAYRINCOURT WOOD.	June 7th (continued)		Repairing roads towards PLACE MONTMARE Q8 d 27.	J.O.
		8ª	As on 7th. Strong party on drainage of trenches and laying duck boards. Tapes out forward trenches from Sap heads.	J.O.
		9ª	As on 8th. Front lines were drained by men not otherwise engaged. Portion of wire on intermediate line taped out.	J.O.
		10ª	As on 9th. Regimental Aid Post (splinter proof shelter) commenced Q3 d 24. Party engaged on clearing dry stream bed of Rieu Trenches at Q10 a 25 to give covered access to firing line. First Flower Pot statue in Sap B.	J.O.
		11ª	As on 10th.	J.O.
		12	As on 11th. Battalions Headquarters @ Q3 c 84 completed. Firing flower pot statues at P18 c 50. Camouflaging covered approach to TRESCAULT. Fitting up dugout as Advanced Dressing Station for RAMC requirements. Signals dug out Q14 d 17 for Commenced @ P18 c 42.	J.O.
		13ª	As on 12th - plus new C.T. Q10 a 0. 5 Q10 c 34 commenced	J.O.
		14	As on 13th. Bn Hdqrs @ Q10 a 44 completed - bunking and fittings. Water Supply Commenced. New C.T. to firing line Q.20 - engine house for new engine completed.	J.O.
		15ª	Hands are all work to 429 Field Coy R.E. and took their work on second line - earthworks on dugouts and C.T. erection of shelters and drainage.	J.O.

1577 Wt. W10791/1773 500,000 1/15 D. D. & L. A.D.S.S./Forms/C. 2118.

WAR DIARY

INTELLIGENCE SUMMARY.

Army Form C. 2118.

(Erase heading not required.)

Place	Date	Hour	Summary of Events and Information	Remarks and references to Appendices
No 1 Sec. YTRES	June (continued)	15th	Sections moved independent. - No 1 Section marching to YTRES. Headquarters	
No 2. "			No.s 2 + 4 Sections to RUYAULCOURT and No 3 to BERTINCOURT. Attached Pioneers	
RUYAULCOURT			moving with each section of R.E.s	J.R.
No 3 "		16th	Sections worked in their own areas on water points standings and drainage of	
BERTINCOURT			same, on hutting, beds, messes, improving, building and siting camps, baths	
			latrines &c. Building incinerators, ablution benches and cookhouses. Dugouts	J.Q.
No 4		17th	for men. DHQ cleared of spoil daily.	J.R.
RUYAULCOURT		18th	Carrying on with all work as on 16th - also on RUYAULCOURT - HERMIES Road	J.R.
Coy Hdqrs		19th	" " " " "	J.Q.
RUYAULCOURT		20th	" " " " "	J.Q.
		21st	" " " " "	J.Q.
		22nd	" " " " "	J.Q.
		23rd	" " " " "	J.Q.
		24th	On 24th - Commenced erection of hessian tents and training shed at BERTINCOURT Jap.	J.Q.
		25	Baths.	J.Q.
		26th	Ballasting of water points at BUS, YTRES, BERTINCOURT, RUYAULCOURT completed. Baths	
			(18 sprays) (hot water) completed at YTRES. Provision of Japanese Baths at	
			BERTINCOURT and BUS commenced.	J.R.

WAR DIARY
INTELLIGENCE SUMMARY

(Erase heading not required.)

Army Form C. 2118.

Place	Date	Hour	Summary of Events and Information	Remarks and references to Appendices
	June	27th	As on 26th	
		28th	As on 27th. Further progress made with (18) Sprengbatt at RUYAULCOURT - with deferred tables at BUS + BERTINCOURT. Work on dugouts in 2nd line, Road to Metting F.C. continued.	F.O F.O
		29th	As on 28th.	F.O
		30th	As on 29th.	F.O

F. Riddich.
MAJOR,
O.C. 428' E.L. Fd. Co. R.E.

428TH
(EAST LANCS.)
FIELD COMPANY, R.E.
No.............
Date 30/6/17

Confidential.
ORIGINAL.

1916

WAR DIARY.
of.
428th (E.L.) Field Company. R.E.

from 1st to 31st July. 1917.

(Volume 4).

WAR DIARY
INTELLIGENCE SUMMARY
(Erase heading not required.)

Army Form C. 2118.

428th (E. Lancs) Field Coy. R.E.

Place	Date	Hour	Summary of Events and Information	Remarks and references to Appendices
	1917.			
Mtd and No 1 Section at YTRES. No 3 Section BERTINCOURT. Hqrs. No 2 & 4 Sections RUYAULCOURT	1st July		Mounted Section and No 1 Section at YTRES, No 3 Section at BERTINCOURT, Hdqrs. No 2 and 4 Sections at RUYAULCOURT — each section having its attached pioneers with it. Each section working independently in its own village area on preparing summer and winter quarters, including baths, ablution benches, incinerators, latrines and such necessaries required for camps, and quarters of officers and men.	
	2nd		As on 1st.	
	3rd		As on 2nd. Nissen hut for lecture hall at D.H.Q. and Sock drying apparatus, attached clean clothing store, both completed.	
	4th		As on 3rd.	
	5th		As on 4th. 3 cookhouses and 9 latrines erected at BUS on new Infantry Battalion site. Preparing to move and handing over papers, sketches, plans and maps to advance Officer of incoming unit, 504th Field Coy. The whole Company moved to YTRES and at night were inspected by General SCHREIBER, C.E. III Corps. After the above No 3 Section returned to BERTINCOURT for the night.	
YTRES	6th		Company (less No 3 Section) and attached pioneers paraded at 6 A.M. for move, marched to le dernois at BUS. Picked up No 3 Section and pioneers there. Company move	

WAR DIARY
or
INTELLIGENCE SUMMARY.

Army Form C. 2118.

Place	Date	Hour	Summary of Events and Information	Remarks and references to Appendices
BUS	6th	(contd)	with 125th Brigade by march route at 7-30 AM, via ROCQUIGNY, LE TRANSLOY and BAPAUME at which place stops. 2 and 4 Sections marched independently to BIHUCOURT	
HQ 2 and 4 BIHUCOURT			and Nos 1 and 3 Sections to GOMIECOURT, each party reaching its respective destination	
Nos 1 and 3 GOMIECOURT			at about 12-30 PM. Company engaged in afternoon erecting its own shelters, also latrines and cleaning up the camp generally.	
	7th		Company engaged on alteration of tracks at ACHIET-LE-PETIT and GOMIECOURT and erecting of tracks at BIHUCOURT. Carried on with erection of own camp quarters, officers quarters, orderly room &c.	
	8th		As on 7th.	
	9th		As on 5th. Strained over all work in ACHIET LE PETIT area to A29 Field Coy.	
	10th		As on 9th. Nos 1 and 3 Sections handed over work at GOMIECOURT to A17 Field Company	
BIHUCOURT			and moved by march route to BIHUCOURT. All attacks pioneer returns to their own battalions.	
	11th		The whole Company moved at 10-40 AM with 126th Brigade by march route to COURCELLES -	
COURCELLES LE COMTE			LE COMTE arriving there at approximately 2-30 PM. Erection of tents, bivouacs, shelters, latrines &c carried on in afternoon	
	12th		Company engaged on 2 Rifle ranges (making new service targets) Cookhouses latrines, mess huts, gallows for bayonet fighting for all 4 battalions. Also improvements to own Company quarters.	

WAR DIARY
or
INTELLIGENCE SUMMARY.
(Erase heading not required.)

Army Form C. 2118.

Place	Date	Hour	Summary of Events and Information	Remarks and references to Appendices
COURCELLES LE COMTE.	13th July 1917		As on 12th with addition of C.E. Church for ACHIET LE PETIT. Work on 300y extra range completed	
	14th		As on 13th	
	15th		As on 14th. Half the Company were re inoculated against Typhoid and so were off duty for 48 hours. Remainder carried on so far as possible with work on foot.	
	16th		As on 15th	
	17th		A 9 days training scheme commenced – each section having its correct proportion in turn of the following :- Squad drill and exercises. Company drill. Instruction in Theatre and Pontoon. Rapid wiring, laying out strong points and fire trenches to Grenade Throwing. Demolitions and Musketry. Each section having one nights instruction on setting out trenches by compass at night. A small number of inaccurately spread out employed men carried on with work.	
	18th		Training as on 18th	
	18th		As on 18th except No 4 who were erecting drying hut for Company's in use and making	
	19th		tables and forms for same.	
	20th		As on 19th	
	21st		As on 20th. Half holiday granted in afternoon	
	22nd		Church Parade in morning	
	23rd		All available ranks for a course of musketry, half Coy in morning and half in afternoon and bayonet fighting instruction given in the half day to those not on musketry	

Army Form C. 2118.

WAR DIARY
or
INTELLIGENCE SUMMARY.
(Erase heading not required.)

Place	Date	Hour	Summary of Events and Information	Remarks and references to Appendices
COURCELLES LE COMTE	24 July		The whole company, less specially employed, engaged in Training as per scheme.	
	25th		Nos 1, 2 and 3 Sections marched to MIRAUMONT Bridging site; leaving COURCELLES LE COMTE at 8 A.M. Employed in erecting a crib pier bridge (for 60 pounder guns) which was not completed by 9 P.M. when the Sections marched back to camp.	
	26th		The whole company marched with tool carts as yesterday to the Bridging grounds and carried on with crib pier, completing same by 5 P.M.	
	27th		Nos 1 and 2 Sections carried on with Training Programme, No 3 to Bridging site where heavy trestle was completed and erected, No 4 Section on 5.9 pr. gun/machine gun dugout for gun and gun team.	
	28th		Party of 16 cyclists dismantled decking of crib pier bridge and returned same to NORD Railway authorities. Trestles practised for the inter-company competition in Rapid Wiring and musketry. Half the company off duty owing to inoculation.	
	29th		Half Company still off duty owing to inoculation. Remainder in Church Parade with Brigade.	
	30th		An 8 days Training Scheme commenced - all four sections on Infantry Drill in early morning Parade and Trestle Bridging, Rapid Wiring musketry, Bayonet fighting &c later. Half Holiday started in afternoon.	
	31st		As on 30th plus demolition of old Boche wire, laying out strong points & loss of members, and loading pack animals (instructions)	

B.F.S.J. Capt. R.E.
O.C. 428th Fd. Coy. R.E.
Major

9157

Confidential.
Original.

WAR DIARY.
of
428th (E. Lancs) Field Coy R.E.
from 1st to 31st August 1917
(Vol. 7)

Army Form C. 2118.

WAR DIARY

INTELLIGENCE SUMMARY.
(Erase heading not required.)

ORIGINAL

Instructions regarding War Diaries and Intelligence Summaries are contained in F. S. Regs., Part II. and the Staff Manual respectively. Title pages will be prepared in manuscript.

428th (E. Lancs.) Field Coy. R.E. Summary of Events and Information 42nd DIVISION.

Place	Date	Hour	Summary of Events and Information	Remarks and references to Appendices
COURCELLES-LE-COMTE	1/8/17		The whole Coy. (less specially employed) attended a lecture given by C.R.E. in the morning on special work of R.E. in the offensive – strong points &c. The whole Coy. (less a few specially employed) paraded at 6.45 p.m. for night operations in accordance with C.R.E.'s scheme and lecture. Pack horses were used for carrying wiring materials from the dumps to where wiring parties required them, and the instructions given for the operation were successfully carried out, and the Coy. returned to Camp in early hours of the morning of the 2nd.	
do.	2/8/17		The Coy. while engaged on Training as per programme, viz:– Musketry, Rapid Wiring, Test of Training, Bridge, Scaling ladders, etc.	
do.	3/8/17		Coy. paraded at 6.45 a.m. carrying midday rations and went out with 126th Infy. Bde. for damp operations in an attack, in accordance with 126th Inf. Bde. Operation Orders.	
do.	4/8/17		Coy. engaged on Training, including Demolitions, etc.	
do.	5/8/17		Church Parades in morning.	
do.	6/8/17		On 9.30 a.m. Parade the whole Company (including special duty men) passed through Gas Test organised by Divl. Gas Officer. The afternoon was devoted to training.	
do.	7/8/17		Coy. paraded at 1.30 p.m. for 126th Bde. Operation Scheme, carrying out an offensive in three different attacks, resulting in the "taking" of COURCELLES-LE-COMTE in the early hours of the 8th. The troops returned to Camp after the operations (which were concluded about 5-30 a.m.) and rested during the morning. Coy. engaged on training in afternoon and preparing for C.R.E.'s inspection.	
do.	8/8/17		Inspection of whole Coy. (on 2nd Parade) & transport equipment and tools, by C.R.E. In the afternoon the Coy. was engaged on training as per scheme.	
do.	9/8/17		Day devoted to training and Baths.	
do.	10/8/17		Company engaged in Training, including especially Gas Drill.	
do.	11/8/17		Church Parades in morning.	
do.	12/8/17		Nos. 1 and 3 Sections, with 2 Lieut. J.P. Cobbin in command went by lorries to GIVENCHY-LE-NOBLE to report at VI Corps Training School to effect repairs on rifle butts. No. 2 Section in training with an Infantry Battalion, and No. 4 M.G. Sergent. Specially employed, working in camp, notably on carriers for pack transport for 126 Brigade.	
do.	13/8/17			

Army Form C. 2118.

WAR DIARY

INTELLIGENCE SUMMARY

(Erase heading not required.)

Instructions regarding War Diaries and Intelligence Summaries are contained in F. S. Regs., Part II. and the Staff Manual respectively. Title pages will be prepared in manuscript.

Place	Date	Hour	Summary of Events and Information	Remarks and references to Appendices
COURCELLES LE COMTE	14-8-17		Hdqrs, Nos 2, & 4 Sections carried on with work in hand — M.G. emplacement & carrier for pack transport and numerous small jobs.	O.C.
do	15-8-17		As on 14th.	do
do	16-8-17		As on 15th.	do
do	17-8-17		Hdqrs, Nos 2 & 4 Sections talking in morning. Experiments made with "BANGALORE" Torpedoes near 208 EAST WOOD.	do
do	18-8-17		Coy. (Hdqrs. 2, & 4 Sections) Red Cross Infantry Drill while wearing Box respirators, drivers wearing them while working on horse lines, and specially employed whilst on duty.	do
do	19-8-17		Hdqrs. & 1st Section (less specially employed) on works principally on pack saddle crates.	do
do	20-8-17		As on 19th. Nos 1 and 3 Sections returned from VI Corps School, GIVENCHY-LE-NOBLE.	do
do	21-8-17		Coy. (including transport) moved by march route from COURCELLES-LE COMTE @ 8.40 A.M. proceeding via BUCQUOY, PUISIEUX-AU-MONT, arriving at its destination, MAILLY-MAILLET, about 2 P.M.	do
MAILLY MAILLET	22-8-17		Coy. rested for the day.	do
BEAUCOURT SUR L'ANCRE	23-8-17		Coy. (including transport) moved by march route @ 5 a.m. from MAILLY-MAILLET to BEAUCOURT sur L'ANCRE where they entrained, leaving at 11 A.M. and arriving at PROVEN bout about 11 pm. The waggons, pontoons, horses, limbers etc were unloaded and the horses harnessed and detrained, and after having a drink of tea the Coy. moved off at about 4 a.m. and marched to WATOU Camp etc.	do
PROVEN				
WATOU	24-8-17			do
WATOU	25-8-17		In morning, Anna inspection Pit. 1800 Respirators were inspected, and mucken parade in afternoon.	do
do	26-8-17		In morning Coy preparing to move to new area, and in afternoon the Coy moved to new camp area.	do
do	27-8-17		Erection of tents and improvements of camp carried on with. All Camera and painting employed to signs & notice boards for new area. Remainder of Coy under section commanders.	do
do	28-8-17		As on 27th.	do
do	29-8-17		As on 28th.	do
do	30-8-17		During morning Coy. were engaged on cleaning up camp and packing transport vehicles prior to moving. Coy moved at 2.15 p.m., marching through POPERINGHE to CHATERTON Siding, where Coy entrained arriving at YPRES about 5 P.M. After entraining, Headquarters Nos 1, 3, & 4 Sections marched to billets allotted to them near MENIN GATE. No. 2 Section & Nounth Section with transport to VLAMERTINGHE.	do
YPRES	31-8-17		Coy employed on cleaning billets, repairing road, draining, building cookhouses etc.	do

J.R. Riddich
Major
O.C. 428th Fd. Coy. R.E.

Vol 8

WAR DIARY
of
428th (E.L.) Field Co. R.E.
from 1st to 30th September 1917.

(Volume 4)

Confidential   ORIGINAL

WAR DIARY / INTELLIGENCE SUMMARY

Army Form C. 2118.

428th (E. Lancs) Field Coy. R.E.

Place	Date	Hour	Summary of Events and Information	Remarks and references to Appendices
MdQ + No 2 Sections VLAMERTINGHE 1, 3 + 4 Sections YPRES. (RAMPARTS)	1917 Sept. 1st		Mounted and No 2 Sections at VLAMERTINGHE Headquarters. No 1, 3 and 4 Sections in Ramparts, South of Menin Gates YPRES. No 1, 3 and 4 Sections engaged on laying duckboard Tracks from Menin Road to Cambridge Road and on from Cambridge Road to FREZENBERG RIDGE, also on billets and drainage of road.	
	2nd		As on 1st. New Orderly Room prepared and erection of coke shelters and ablution house carried on with. Two strong points were taped out & been dug ready for excavation.	
	3rd		As on 2nd.	
	4th		As on 3rd. Only ½ hours work on strong points. Parties engaged on taking wiring materials from Y Dump FREZENBERG RIDGE to LOW FARM.	
	5th		As on 4th. Completion of wiring materials moved to LOW FARM. 1 Officer, 8 sappers and 50 pioneers took part in attack on BORRY FARM. This R.E. party did not however leave LOW FARM until night of 6/7 when the wiring parties under R.E. supervision erected 150 yards of wire.	
	6th		As on 5th.	
	7th		Improved Gas Blanket screen of RAMPARTS including own (Coy) billets, BH.Q + R.A. 2dqs. Shelters for cookers for Right Support batt. site cleared ready for sandbagging. Work carried on on F + J Tracks - duckboards laid & signboards erected.	
	8th		As on 7th plus fitting gas curtain and protecting entrance doorway of concrete shelter at WILDE WOOD Battalion HQ. No 2 Section commenced repairs and additions to existing Broad farming No 2 mule track from MENIN ROAD to CAMBRIDGE ROAD.	
	9th		As on 8th. Work on strong points postponed indefinitely owing to lack of working parties.	
	10th		On on 9th. Reconnaissance completed for F Track from CAMBRIDGE ROAD westwards to MENIN ROAD. 100 yds additional duckboards laid on J Track, No 2 mule Track ready for use up to CAMBRIDGE ROAD.	

Army Form C. 2118.

WAR DIARY
INTELLIGENCE SUMMARY.
(Erase heading not required.)

Instructions regarding War Diaries and Intelligence Summaries are contained in F.S. Regs., Part II. and the Staff Manual respectively. Title pages will be prepared in manuscript.

Place	Date	Hour	Summary of Events and Information	Remarks and references to Appendices
	11th Sept.		100 yds additional duckboarding laid on F Track, 200 yds on J Track, chiefly east of IBEX Trench. Site for 2 battalion cookers camouflaged and sandbagging proceeding. Work on the 2 mule tracks WILDE WOOD, and LOW FARM carried on with.	J.R.
	12		As on 11th. 180 yds duckboarding laid on J Track. Sandbag buttress in front of entrance had bursting course over same completed at WILDE WOOD Bn. HQ. Repairs to LOW FARM concrete shelter carried on and 2 OP's made and approach trench cut. Material for 450 yds wire entanglement moved up to Y Dump.	J.R.
	13th		Duckboarding F & J Tracks. Laying roadway on No 2 Mule Track. Men got proceeding made of old german concrete shelters on FREZENBERG RIDGE. Assembly trenches taped out for infantry on right and left sectors of front line.	J.Q.
	14th		Battalion over work on F & J Tracks to 90 Field Coy (9th Division) Carried on with Ag 2 Mule Tracks. Repairs to WILDE WOOD Bn. HQ. Roads to tape out new front line trenches between SANS SOUCI and Railway, F Track moved out from CAMBRIDGE ROAD to MENIN ROAD.	J.R.
	15th		Preparing for move on morning of 16 to BRANDHOEK. Surplus stores moved by rail or trap. and limber.	J.Q.
BRANDHOEK.	16th		Company moved from RAMPARTS, YPRES by march route at 9.20 arriving at Horse Lines Camp. BRANDHOEK @ 11 AM.	J.R.
	17th		Company vehicles washed and painted. Men tested in afternoon lecture (all men) by No 3 Section.	J.R.
	18th		3 Officers 65 OR (cavalry) @ 3.30 AM and proceeded by motor lorries to the Ramparts to work in camouflaging the MENIN ROAD. Remainder of Coy on special duties, including painting & washing of vehicles.	J.Q.
	19th		Company transport and cyclists tradesmen parcelled @ 7.45 AM and moved by march route per BRANDHOEK. Remainder of Coy. were moved by motor lorries via POPERINGHE to WINNEZEELE & on arriving here about 10.30 AM. Transport personnel marching in about 1 PM.	J.R.
WINNEZEELE.				

Army Form C. 2118.

WAR DIARY
INTELLIGENCE SUMMARY.
(Erase heading not required.)

Instructions regarding War Diaries and Intelligence Summaries are contained in F.S. Regs., Part II. and the Staff Manual respectively. Title pages will be prepared in manuscript.

Place	Date	Hour	Summary of Events and Information	Remarks and references to Appendices
WINNEZEELE	20th Sept		Infantry Training and Kit Inspection in morning	K.R.
WORMHOUDT	21st		Company moved much route from WINNEZEELE about 10 AM arriving at WORMHOUDT @ 3 pm	K.R.
	22nd		Company from WORMHOUDT by much route and 8 AM arriving at TETEGHEM area billets at about 2 pm	K.R.
TETEGHEM AREA	23rd		Coy moved from TETEGHEM by much route to LE PANNE about 1 pm	K.R.
LE PANNE	24th		Coy moved from LE PANNE to much Nortr. Machine Gun billets at LE PANNE about 2 nom. taking over from A20 Field Coy R.E. (66th Division)	K.R.
OOST DUNKERQUE BAINS	25th		No 3 Section available for camp duties. No 1 & No 2 on repairs and upkeep of Roads. No 3 on upkeep of Railways. No 4 moved up to forward billets at ROUGHTON and took on upkeep of Tramway and extension of same towards R. Bn. HQ.	K.R.
	26th		As on 25th. Nol Section to No 1 Section R. Bn. HQ	K.R.
	27th		As on 26th	K.R.
	28th		As on 27th	K.R.
	29th		As on 28th. Mounted Section moved with vehicles (excluding Tool carts Funk cart) to OXYDE.	K.R.
	30th		BAINS at 7 PM under Captain BUTTON. Work for dismounted sections as on 29th.	K.R.

428TH
(EAST LANCS.)
FIELD COMPANY, R.E.

J. Riddick Major
O.C. 428th Fd. Coy. R.E.

WAR DIARY.

of

428th (E. Lancs) Field Coy. R.E.

from 1st to 31st October. 1917.

(Volume 4).

Army Form C. 2118.

WAR DIARY
~~INTELLIGENCE SUMMARY~~
(Erase heading not required.)

ORIGINAL

Instructions regarding War Diaries and Intelligence Summaries are contained in F. S. Regs., Part II. and the Staff Manual respectively. Title pages will be prepared in manuscript.

428th (East Lancs) Field Co. R.E.

Place	Date	Hour	Summary of Events and Information	Remarks and references to Appendices
No. 4 Section ROUGHTOWN	1st Oct.		No. 4 Section in forward billets at Roughtown, Hdqrs. Nos. 1, 2, 3 Sections at OOST DUNKERKE BAINS, Mounted Section at ST. IDESBALDE. No. 4 Section on work on Kanyong – extension dam to right battalion sector. No. 1 Section on work for R.A. – on Shelters, O.P's dugouts etc. No. 2 Section on road repair, and No. 3 on repairing and improving subways.	
Hdqs. Nos. 1, 2 & 3 Sections	2nd "		As on 1st. Thunder over work on roads to 6th Bn. Kidel Regt. Reserve.	
OOST-DUNKERKE BAINS.	3rd "		As on 2nd. No. 2 Section in erection of elephant shelters in camp for use of Company.	
MOUNTED SECTION – ST IDESBALDE	4th "		As on 3rd. 2 Officers of 237th Field Coy. R.E. (41st Div.) taken round works & subway jobs.	
	5th "		Our advance parties were taken round 219th Field Coy. R.E. (32nd Div.) works & jobs. Parties of N.C.Os. from 237th Field Coy. R.E. taken round the various jobs in Kem. viz: Existing O.P's and Subways. Work carried on as on 4th.	
H.Q. WULPEN	6th "		Company handed over forward (ROUGHTOWN) and OOST DUNKERKE BAINS billets to 237th Field Coy. R.E. At 2.30 p.m. Company and attached Riviera Kennel & move by march route to WULPEN, taking over forward & back billets of 219th Field Coy. R.E. Headquarters, No. 1 & 2 Sections taking over new billets & No. 2 & 3 Sections and attached infantry taking over forward billets. Coy. arrived at new billets at 4.30 p.m., and at dusk Nos. 2 & 3 Sections with their attached infantry moved to take over forward billets (TRICAR MAISON)	
"	7th "		Nos. 2 and 3 Sections at forward billets. No. 1 Section on reconning pontoon from the Canal and bringing them to WULPEN CAMP. Nos. 2 Section parades & 3 Sections parades to forward billets joining Nos. 2 and 3 Sections.	

Army Form C. 2118.

WAR DIARY
or
INTELLIGENCE SUMMARY.
(Erase heading not required.)

Instructions regarding War Diaries and Intelligence Summaries are contained in F.S. Regs., Part II. and the Staff Manual respectively. Title pages will be prepared in manuscript.

Place	Date	Hour	Summary of Events and Information	Remarks and references to Appendices
Hqrs. NULPEN	8th Oct.		No. 1 Section engaged on cleaning and improving billets. Nos. 2, 3 and 4 on maintenance & repair of bridges. Regimental Aid Post, camouflaging TRICAR R.E. Dump, assisting Infantry on Bn. Batt. front to lay duckboards in F.T.'s and C.T.'s, working on TRICAR S.P. - wiring proceeding. - Two M.G. emplacements in hand.	J.E.
"	9th "		As on 8th.	J.E.
"	10th "		As on 9th. One gets carried out in NULPEN billets - making repairing cupboards, improving billets with tarred felting, repair of cycles, etc.	J.E.
"	11th "		As on 10th.	J.E.
"	12th "		As on 11th. Repairs carried out to RAMSCAPELLE ROAD and duckboard track. Screens erected and duckboards laid along canal side.	J.E.
"	13th "		As on 12th.	J.E.
"	14th "		As on 13th. No. 1 Section move from NULPEN camp billets to forward billets at TRICAR MILL and took over No. 4 Section's dugouts. No. 4 Section moving back to No. 1 Section's vacated billets.	J.E.
"	15th "		As on 14th. Work on TRICAR S.P. postponed, by order of Bde. Work commenced on two emplacements and shelters in NUN WALK. Duckboards laid, principally on left Battalion front, owing to it being much worn. Most Right Battalion front. Moving buildings from roof of forward Battn. Hqrs. spotting in place. Cement 1'6" thick. Repairing bridges as they become damaged by shell fire etc.	J.E.
"	16th "		As on 15th. Bridges repaired as soon after being damaged as possible.	J.E.
"	17th "		As on 16th. No. 4 Section to Divl. R.E. Dump, workshops.	J.E.
"	18th "		As on 17th.	J.E.
"	19th "		As on 18th. Collecting Elephant Shelters and timber for Gum Boot Drying Room and Foot Drying Room.	J.E.
WHITE HOUSE	20th "		As on 19th. Filling in Shell holes.	J.E.

A5834. Wt. W4973/M687 750,000 8/16 D.D. & L. Ltd. Forms/C2118/13.

Army Form C. 2118.

WAR DIARY
or
INTELLIGENCE SUMMARY.
(Erase heading not required.)

Instructions regarding War Diaries and Intelligence Summaries are contained in F.S. Regs. Part II. and the Staff Manual respectively. Title pages will be prepared in manuscript.

Place	Date	Hour	Summary of Events and Information	Remarks and references to Appendices
H.Q. HULPEN	21st Oct		As on 20th.	
"	22nd "		As on 21st.	
"	23rd "		As on 22nd.	
"	24th "		As on 23rd. Duckboarding and draining in NUN and NICE AVENUES and NICE WALKS. Construction of 2 M.G. Shelters in NUN and NICE WALKS carried on with. NASTY WALKS. Excavating position for H.Q. at NORA POST.	
"	25th "		Reinforcing earling shelter (damaged by shell fire) in support line. Work on Gun Boat Slope carried on with, also hot drying room. No. 7 Section moved from Dnit. R.E. Wortestops & relieve No. 3 Section at Forman Huith. - No. 3 taking over posts on hand at Dnit. R.E. Wortestops.	
"	26th "		As on 25th. Repairs to bridge damaged by enemy shell fire carried out. Covering of Boys Shelter at Forman Huith at TRICAR proceeded with.	
"	27th "		As on 26th. Erecting of M.G. emplacements at MAISON HARDY and BRICKSTACKS completed.	
"	28th "		As on 27th. Reserve heavy dumps were made for "ELIZABETH"(2) and "ALBERT"(1) BRIDGES and ant forming.	
"	29th "		As on 28th.	
"	30th "		Duckboarding of NICE AVENUE completed. Work on new O.P. carried out.	
"	31st "		Various jobs to trust proceeded with. Field Coy. Commander conferred with O.P.E. on subject of maintenance and demolition of bridges.	

428TH
(EAST LANCS.)
FIELD COMPANY, R.E.
No.
Date 31/10/17

/ O.C. 428th Fd. Coy. R.E.

M 10

WAR DIARY.

of

428th (E1) Field Co. R.E.

from 1st to 30th Nov. 1917.

(Volume 4)

Confidential
ORIGINAL

Army Form C. 2118.

WAR DIARY
or
INTELLIGENCE SUMMARY.
(Erase heading not required.)

ORIGINAL

Place	Date	Hour	Summary of Events and Information	Remarks and references to Appendices
Coy. Hdqrs. WULPEN. No. 4 Section at Div. R.E. Dump. Nos. 1, 2 & 3 Sections at forward billets MAISON TRICAR Mounted Section 1 Q.M. Stores KERKPANNE.	1/9/17		428th (E. LANCS) FIELD COMPANY. R.E. Duckboarding and draining in NUN and NICE AVENUES, NICE WALK, NUN STREET, and NUN WALK carried on with. Renovation of M.G. Shelters. NICE and NUN walks, M.G. Emplacement, BRICKSTACKS completed. O.P. at VETERINAIRE - Concreting carried on with. K.G. position, NORA POST, - excavation completed, ready for concreting. Renewing existing Shelter in Support line. Gum Boot Store at MAISON BRANCHE &c. Screening of BRUGES ROAD. Repairing of bridges as they become damaged carried on with.	J.R. J.R.
	2/9/17		Duckboarding and draining in NUN and NICE AVENUES and NUN STREET completed. Concreting commenced on K.G. position, NORA POST. Div. O.P. roof damaged by shell fire and repairs at night. Concreting of Fd. Bde. &c. completed and sandbagging carried on with. Floating bridge near PELICAN BRIDGE taken to WULPEN for repair.	J.R. J.R.
	3/9/17		As on 2nd.	
	4/9/17		As on 3rd. No. 4 Section moved from R.E. Dump to relieve No. 2 Section, who, on being relieved at TRICAR marched down to the Div. R.E. Dump. (Workshops). Bridge No. 53 moved 30' at request of B.M.	J.R. J.R.
	5/9/17		As on 4th.	J.R.
	6/9/17		As on 5th.	J.R.
	7/9/17		As on 6th. No. 2 Section (workshops section) relieved by section of 429th Field Coy. R.E. who took over jobs on hand at the Workshops and No. 2 Sect. moved to Regl Billets (WULPEN).	J.R.
	8/9/17		As on 7th. Building up parapet, putting in U. Frames & relaying Duckboards in NUN AVENUE for a length of 40'.	J.R.
	9/9/17		As on 8th. Screening of NICE AVENUE at its junction with NICE WALK completed. Repair of screen N. of ALBERT BRIDGE completed. Sandbagging on Field Survey Coy. Dugout completed. O.P. VETERINAIRE tunnel, also erection of a WIRE Breakwater in screen carried out. Concreting roof and sides, repairing loose windows &c. of Gum BOOT STORE proceeded with. Erection of 5 Elephant Shelters for Adv. 1 Bde Hq. at BRIQUETTERIE commenced.	J.R. J.R.
	10/9/17		As on 9th. Erecting additional stabling & improving roads & drains at Coy. Transport Lines Camp.	J.R.
	11/9/17		As on 10th. Advanced B.H.Q. ready for concreting.	J.R.

Army Form C. 2118.

ORIGINAL

WAR DIARY or INTELLIGENCE SUMMARY.

(Erase heading not required.)

Instructions regarding War Diaries and Intelligence Summaries are contained in F.S. Regs. Part II. and the Staff Manual respectively. Title pages will be prepared in manuscript.

Place	Date	Hour	Summary of Events and Information	Remarks and references to Appendices
	12/7/17		Consulting of Advanced B.H.Q. carried on with	J.O.
	13/7/17		As on 11th	J.O.
	14/7/17		As on 12th	J.O.
	15/7/17		As on 13th	J.O.
	16/7/17		As on 15th. Advanced B.H.Q. (Elephant Shelter) completed, and accepted by Bde Staff. Advance party from French Divn. showen round billets, stores, etc.	J.O.
	17/7/17		As on 16th. No.1 and 4 Sections sent attached pioneers moved from TRICAR Billets to Coy. H.Q. (WULPEN) Billets. Preparing for move - all surplus kit over & room forces, baggage, stores, etc. transported to Railhead, (ST. IDESBALDE) to be sent on by train.	J.O.
	18/7/17		As on 17th.	J.O.
WORMHOUDT	19/7/17		Coy. moved by march route from WULPEN billets (including 126th M.G.C. & 126th L.T.M.B.) passing through DUNKERTE at 6 A.M., hence through COXYDE, KERKPANNE, OOSTDOEK, to ADINKERKE where column entrained at 9 A.M. for BERGUES, - hence by march route to WORMHOUDT area "A". Coy transport moved all through by road.	J.O.
	20/7/17		Coy. moved by march route at 1 p.m. from WORMHOUDT area A to area B, the billets being situated half way between RIETVELD and ZERMEZEELE.	J.O.
EBBLINGHEM	21/7/17		Coy. moved by march route at 8.15 a.m. (under Bde. arrangements) the starting point being WEMAERS CAPPEL, passing on western edge of CASSEL in to EBBLINGHEM area	J.O.
CLOMENGHEM	22/7/17		Coy. moved by march route from EBBLINGHEM (starting at 8-30 A.M.) to CLOMENGHEM, in the AIRE district.	J.O.
	23/7/17		Coy. fixed up in billets. Inspection of ammo and gas equipment carried out in morning, and kit inspection on afternoon parade.	J.O.
	24/7/17		Bridging vehicle unloaded, and all Coy. vehicles washed. Signs painted on where necessary. Baths arranged for the men, under Coy. management.	J.O.
	25/7/17		As on 24th	J.O.
	26/7/17		As on 25th. Washing and painting of Coy. vehicles completed ready for inspection. Everything prepared & advanced ready for early move on 27th.	J.O.
ROBECQ	27/7/17		Coy. moved by march route from CLOMENGHEM at 8.30 A.M. passing through RINCQ, AIRE, ST. VENANT & BUSNES arriving to ROBECQ. Were at approx. 2 p.m. moving into billets allotted to Coy for the night.	J.O.
ESSARS	28/7/17		Coy. moved by march route, leaving ROBECQ at 8-45 A.M. to ESSARS (via BETHUNE) arriving at destination about 1 p.m.	J.O.

Army Form C. 2118.

WAR DIARY
or
INTELLIGENCE SUMMARY.
(Erase heading not required.)

ORIGINAL

Place	Date	Hour	Summary of Events and Information	Remarks and references to Appendices
ESSARS	29/1/17		No.1 Section moved to Divl. R.E. Workshops at GORRE, taking over work in hand there. Remainder of Coy. in cleaning and painting of vehicle and removing Coy. Stores &c. from dump at Ecole de filo, BETHUNE.	
	30/1/17		Nos 2, 3 and 4 Sections on work on Stores Lines, including erection of troughs &c. After work was completed three the sections were Paraded in Drill Order for Rifle Exercises &squad & Communication Drill. This was also carried out on afternoon.	

J. Riddick
Major
O.C. 428th Fd. Coy. R.E.

428TH
(EAST LANCS.)
FIELD COMPANY, R.E.
No. ....
Date 30/1/17

Vol 11

WAR DIARY
of
428th (E.L.) 2nd en R.E.
from 1st to 31st December 1917

(Volume 4)

Confidential
ORIGINAL

Army Form C. 2118.

ORIGINAL

WAR DIARY
INTELLIGENCE SUMMARY.
(Erase heading not required.)

Instructions regarding War Diaries and Intelligence Summaries are contained in F.S. Regs., Part II. and the Staff Manual respectively. Title pages will be prepared in manuscript.

Place	Date	Hour	Summary of Events and Information	Remarks and references to Appendices
ESSARS & LE QUESNOY	1-12-17		428TH (East Lancs) FIELD COY. R.E. Headquarters Nos. 2, 3 & 4 Sections and Mounted station at ESSARS. No.1 Section at LE QUESNOY, being R.E. Workshops Section, Divl. Dump BORRE. Nos. 2, 3 & 4 Sections on repair to refilling sheds for Divl 7, 3 Bdes, work at Batt. Hq tote line, repairs to bathing apparatus, stoves rotava at D.H.Q., boot drying room at BORRE. 1 Officer detached for Tramway work, as Divisional Tramway Officer.	J.R.
	2-12-17		As on 1st. Work in stables at D.H.Q. completed.	J.R.
	3-12-17		As on 2nd. Mounted Section moved to fresh quarters situated at LE QUESNOY. Coy. vehicles being cleaned & oiled, ready for painting. Erection of boxes for Horse Lines at 19 K.M.V.S. completed.	J.R.
LE QUESNOY	4-12-17		As on 3rd. Nos. 2 & 3 rd Sections moved from ESSARS by march route to new billets at LE QUESNOY — the whole Coy. (including Mounted Section) being in the one area. Pump at BEUVRY Baths inspected.	J.R.
	5-12-17		As on 4th. A new pump and inspection at BEUVRY baths, & the one returned to R.E. Dump 120 Infty. Brigade Workshops.	J.R.
	6-12-17		As on 5th. Work on shaft laying in room completed. No.3 Section moved by march route to HINGETTE-LES CAUDRONS area to work on billets to accommodate on battalion by 9th inst.	J.R.
	7-12-17	6 A.M.		J.R.
	8-12-17	7½		J.R.
	9-12-17	8½	Erection of shelter for pipe rotava at BEUVRY Baths commenced.	J.R.
	10-12-17	9½	No. 3 Section withdrawn from LES CAUDRONS — work on Batt Billets completed. Construction of workshops at 42nd Divl Wing commenced. Arrangements made for bathing men for not work.	J.R.
	11-12-17	10 K	Structure for protection of rations of 126 F.A.Bde commenced. Work for R.A. concerning gun pits, erection of elephant shelters, and repairs carried on with.	J.R.
	12-12-17	11 th	Work commenced on erection of covered horse line to accommodate 20 horses for 19th M.V.S. 3 stores being made for huts at LES CAUDRONS. Work on tramway (Ballasting, drainage, & extension of line) carried on with.	J.R.
	13-12-17	12 th	Pump at BEUVRY (Billet 155) & at BEUVRY Baths both repaired. 2 stoves made further in billets at LES CAUDRONS.	J.R.
	14-12-17	13 th	As on 13th. All 3 stoves fitted at LES CAUDRONS. Repairs to screen on LA BASSEE ROAD & HARLEY ST. north of WINDY CORNER carried out.	J.R.
	15-12-17	14 th	Divl. Salvage Officer interviewed as to erection of incinerator for extracting lead from tins. Billet for pipe rotava at BEUVRY BATHS completed. Work on Bath billets at BEUVRY well advanced, repair assistance withdrawn. Two elephant shelters completed for R.A. Battery.	J.R.

Army Form C. 2118.

ORIGINAL

WAR DIARY

INTELLIGENCE SUMMARY
(Erase heading not required.)

SHEET. 2.

Place	Date	Hour	Summary of Events and Information	Remarks and references to Appendices
LE QUESNOY	16-12-17		As on 15th. Work over from 429th Field Coy. R.E. erection of concrete shelters near WINDY CORNER	9.Q
	17-12-17		As on 16th	9.Q
	18-12-17		As on 17th. Div. Divisional Survey Officer handed over work in hand to Officer of 429th Fd. Coy. R.E. who takes over this post. Work on Baynes, Mess etc. at LE PREON completed. Work completed on ovens & ammunition dump (near ESTAMINET CORNER)	9.A 9.Q
	19-12-17		As on 18th. Work on 126 x 2 Inf. Brigade supply shed completed. 1 Officer & small party of N.C.O's taken over jobs in hand by 427th Fd. Coy. R.E.	9.Q
	20-12-17		As on 19th. Small parties again taken over 427 Fd.Coy for additional stores put in huts at D.H.Q. New standings (& roads) for 428th Field Coy. R.E. completed. Erection of stoke amm'n. shelters, & drying room in Gun Boot shore, including gas-proof doors & curtains in carpenters hut, completed.	9.Q
	21-12-17		As on 20th. Standing over to 427 Fd. Coy. R.E. Work on maintenance of trenches, excavation for concrete shelters, T.M. Emplacements etc. carried on with. Erection work on B.H.Q.	9.Q
	22-12-17		As on 21st. R.E. completed. (Work on working parties transport taken over from 427 Coy. R.E. wiring completed.	9.Q
	23-12-17		As on 22nd.	9.Q
	24-12-17		" 23rd, except night parties, which were cancelled.	9.Q
	25-12-17		All work with parties cancelled - this day for the troops all day	9.Q
	26-12-17		As on 23rd. Repairs to MOND RAIL carried on with.	9.Q
	24-12-17		" 26th. Erection of camouflage frames receive for pits of 6" T.M. Emplacements completed. Excavation work for various concrete shelters progressing favourably.	9.Q
	28-12-17		As on 27th.	9.A
	29-12-17		" 28th.	9.A
	30-12-17		" 29th. Commence something for SPOILBANK concrete shelters.	9.A
	31-12-17		" 3rd. 36 Private of 1/5th S. LANCS Regt. reported for work. They kept in hand excavation for Pill Box 16.2 in TOWER RESERVE & the provision of S.A.A. Bomb & Ration stores for the 6 Keeps in Brigade Front.	9.A

J. Riddich
D.O. 429th Fd. Coy. R.E.

9012

Confidential
ORIGINAL

WAR DIARY

of

428th (East Lancs) Field Coy. R.E.

from 1st to 31st January. 1918

(Volume 5)

Army Form C. 2118.

WAR DIARY

~~INTELLIGENCE SUMMARY~~

(Erase heading not required.)

ORIGINAL

428TH FIELD COMPANY, R.E.

Place	Date	Hour	Summary of Events and Information	Remarks and references to Appendices
LE QUESNOY	1-1-18		Work in hand :— Excavation of concrete shelters and pill boxes carried on with. Concreting commenced on KINGSCLERE PARRY ARGOSIE SHELTER. S.A.A. water & Replin Stores in Keeps proceeded with. Gas Blankets being fitted in dugouts. The moving up of gravel to forward area from PONT FIXE R.E. Dump carried out as previously.	
	2-1-18		Work on T.M.B. tunnels, SIDBURY HILL & at Screen Post 6"T.M's. proceeded with.	A.2.
	3-1-18		As on 1st. S.A.A. store at SPOIL BANK KEEP completed.	A.2.
	4-1-18		As on 2nd. Erection of gas curtains & pump in Coy. H.Q. OXFORD TERRACE completed. Repairing & lagging of pumps proceeded with.	A.2.
	5-1-18		As on 4th. Repairs to KINGSWAY & MARYLEBONE taken in hand.	A.2.
	6-1-18		As on 5th. Signwriters repainters on painting & re-writing of various signs. All concreting in abeyance owing to heavy frost.	A.2.
	7-1-18		As on 6th.	A.2.
	8-1-18		As on 7th.	A.2.
	9-1-18		As on 8th. Camouflage extended & improved on ORCHARD KEEP & SPOIL BANK KEEP Concrete shelters.	A.2.
	10-1-18		As on 9th. 3 forward R.E. dumps 80% equipped with materials ordered.	A.2.
	11-1-18		As on 10th. Shelters for S.A.A. bombs, water & rations completed at SPOIL BANK and ORCHARD Keeps. Dugout entrance to BRADDELL KEEP re-timbered. Concreting commenced on Nos. 1 & 2 Concrete Shelters OXFORD TERRACE, and on N°3 Concrete Shelter ORCHARD KEEP. Commenced fixing fine wire facing frames & rear in the different localities on Left Bn. Reserve Line (N. of Canal)	A.2.
	12-1-18		As on 11th.	A.2.
	13-1-18		As on 12th.	A.2.
	14-1-18		As on 13th.	A.2.
	15-1-18		As on 14th.	A.2.
	16-1-18		Owing to an entire change of weather conditions, and a sudden thaw setting in, concreting work in all instances is in abeyance and all available men employed in clearing trenches, duckboarding & revetting. Most of the precautions for concrete shelters are now full of water & in some cases nearly fell of the walls have taken place.	A.2.
	17-1-18		150 men from flour Brigade put at my disposal for cleaning mud out of trenches. Chiefly employed on night C.T. & main line of resistance. Work on gas blankets continued to tunnel entrances & repairs to pumps proceeded with.	A.2.
	18-1-18		As on 17th. Cleaning trenches. KINGSWAY, THE LANE, MARYLEBONE, ESPERANTO TERRACE, COLDSTREAM LANE EAST & WEST & GRAFTON ST. continued.	A.2.

Army Form C. 2118.

WAR DIARY
INTELLIGENCE SUMMARY.
(Erase heading not required.)

Instructions regarding War Diaries and Intelligence Summaries are contained in F.S. Regs., Part II. and the Staff Manual respectively. Title pages will be prepared in manuscript.

ORIGINAL

Place	Date	Hour	Summary of Events and Information	Remarks and references to Appendices
	19-1-18.		As on 15th. Additional 120 O.R. of South Lancs Regt. (Pioneers) allotted to me for work on trench repairs.	2/L M
	20-1-18.		As on 19th. 3 Section 423rd Field Coy. R.E. with 50 Infantry details by C.R.E. to assist in trench repairs on Right Res. Sector.	2/L M
	21-1-18.		As on 20th.	2/L M
	22-1-18.		As on 21st. All working parties employed on trench cutting (chiefly of parados) at night — clearing mud & clearing duckboards by day. Clearing of fatta gutting well in hand.	"
	23-1-18.		As on 22nd.	"
	24-1-18.		No new mud has been cleared. Efforts concentrated on drainage of trenches on left Bn. front.	"
	25-1-18.		As on 24th. Commenced cleaning abandoned A.D.S. tunnels in SPOIL BANK with a view to trucking for spares for some of garrison of BAYSWATER.	"
	26-1-18.		As on 25th. Concreting recommenced at No. 1. Concrete Shelter. SPOIL BANK KEEP. S. Lancs. Pioneers commenced berm cutting on side of WILLOW DRAIN between FINCHLEY Rd. and ORCHARD ROAD.	"
	27-1-18.		As on 26th. CAMBRIDGE TERRACE cleared of water. Puncturing of worst places of ORCHARD RD, FINCHLEY RD & CAMBRIDGE TERRACE commenced — constant pumping necessary.	"
	28-1-18.		As on 27th. New C.T. (Communication Trench) between ORCHARD ROAD & CHEYNE WALK made passable — Orchard Drain reconstructing proceeding.	"
	29-1-18.		No working parties owing to the Brigade relief. Most urgent work carried on with assistance of attached infantry.	"
	30-1-18.		Concreting proceeding in Spoilbank Keep Shelter. Parties detailed to repair FINCHLEY Rd., ORCHARD Rd. & CAMBRIDGE TERRACE. Started all night trucking at front line from FINCHLEY Rd. to CRATER POST.	"
	31-1-18		As on 30th. S. Lancs Pioneers on MARYLEBONE, WILLOW DRAIN & FINCHLEY Rd. Commenced whalloasting with brick hand-car from SUDBURY HILL to GUNNER TRENCH.	"

428TH
(EAST LANCS.)
FIELD COMPANY, R.E.
No. ....
Date 31-1-18

J. Middich, Major
O.C. 428th Fd. Coy. R.E.

Vol 13

War Diary.

of
428th (E. Lancs) Field Coy. RE.

from 1st to 28th February. 1916.

(Volume 5).

Confidential
ORIGINAL

WAR DIARY

Army Form C. 2118.

ORIGINAL

(Erase heading not required)

Place	Date	Hour	Summary of Events and Information	Remarks and references to Appendices
LE QUESNOY	1-2-18		428th FIELD COMPANY R.E. Carrying proceeding on Spoil Bank Keep Shelter. Started all night pumping out front line from FINCHLEY ROAD to CRATER POST. South Lane. Ponies on WILLOW DRAIN and duckboard maint. and revetting commenced. re-laying tramway track from SIDBURY HILL to GUNNER TRENCH. Completed shell holes behind CRATER POST and believed much water. Defence facilities produced. KINGSWAY and TOWER RESERVE. Night parties continued berm cutting in paradoes. As on 1/2.	
	2-2-18		Manage amongst Coy. horses now assuming grave aspect.	
	3-2-18		Work on FINCHLEY and ORCHARD ROADS proceeded all day. WILLOW DRAIN deepened and rivetted at	
	4-2-18		North end. Company horses much depleted in strength. Work on BAYSWATER & Berm cutting in	
	5-2-18		Right Redoubt. Front Line. clearing continued. Company Lorries visited by D.A.D.V.S. and A.D.V.S. 1st Corps. All horses now examined except 19. All precautions taken. Near horses, eruptive completely isolated. All defective localities of Right Bank. marked in company with B.M. 125 Bde. & works proceeding as or at. Schemes revised with D.G.O. & arrangements made for properly	
	6-2-18		protecting Gunner End. A.A. & Q.M.G. inspected Transport Lines. All Mounted Details clothing fumigated. Same as head of FINCHLEY ROAD. Blown in by T.M. fire. repaired at night. Visited Localities N. of Canal with Q/6.O.C. 125 Inf. Bde.	
	7-2-18		Arrangements made for all horses to be clipped on Sunday next. Meanwhile horses are being dressed daily with solution of sulphur-grease.	
	8-2-18		No parties. Few Sappers on works remainder on gas drill/bathing and clean clothing. A.D.V.S. called revealed that precautions taken by us were all that in	
	9-2-18		required. Work as on 7/2. QUEEN'S ROAD and WARRINGTON LANE now in good order. Damage to	
	10-2-18		FINCHLEY ROAD by enemy T.M. fire. - repairs at night. As on 9/2.	
	11-2-18		As on 10/2. Attached Infantry left the Coy. to rejoin their respective battalions.	

Army Form C. 2118.

WAR DIARY
INTELLIGENCE SUMMARY
(Erase heading not required.)

ORIGINAL

Instructions regarding War Diaries and Intelligence Summaries are contained in F. S. Regs., Part II. and the Staff Manual respectively. Title pages will be prepared in manuscript.

Place	Date	Hour	Summary of Events and Information	Remarks and references to Appendices
LE QUESNOY	12-2-18		NCO's from Hy 423rd Fd Coy RE visiting lines with men of this Coy preparatory to taking over. Stock lists of all dumps prepared. GRE snapshots shown. Lines reported on methods.	
	13-2-18		Handing over to relieving unit continued. W.P.S as usual. All gas plants have returned regiment. Fd. 423rd Fd Coy took over all drawings, plans, and petition systems in line in Hd. 13ode Area. 4 more lorries available.	
	14-2-18		Training commenced 9 am. Squad Drill, Gas Drill 12 noon. Training ceased on instruction from CE I Corps of defence work in SAILLY, NOYELLES CAMBRIN and NOEUX. 1 Company & 1mn Pioneer Battalion (North Inn) to be attached to Coy, to live in SAILLY. 1 Officer + 23 ORs to Remount Depot, BOULOGNE for 76 remounts.	
	15-2-18		Officer + NCO's reconnoitred new work. Arrangements for work, supply of materials, etc. made with S.O.R.E. I Corps.	
	16-2-18		Work commenced on tunnelled dugouts at SAILLY POST, CAMBRIN, also on 2 OP's at FOSSE NOEUX-LES-MINES. Also on strengthening cellar at NOYELLES. One Coy North Umfrs commenced work to-day. Preparation of maps undertaken in connection with dugouts.	
	17-2-18		No 3 Section moved into billets at SAILLY, for commence whilst working at the NOEUX mining mnd O.P.s 2 Pionrs officers attached to Coy for instruction. Tunnelling proceeding at SAILLY POST and CAMBRIN.	
	18-2-18		Excellent progress at SAILLY and CAMBRIN. Other works in hand carried on with.	
	19-2-18		Struck water at SAILLY 11 am. Designs settled at once. Decided to put in C Type Elephant Dugout from dugout. 46 Remounts arrived. Work as on 18.2.	
	20-2-18		CE and CAMBRIN DUGOUT and did not like entrance. No 3 OP at CAMBRIN started yesterday. To be commenced at once, and site chosen about 40x from strong point on 20 ft wiring carried at NOEUX worthy partly lowered over to 17 ft.	
	21-2-18		All stores dipped at BETHUNE. Harrassmentsyrr. Tunnelling by RE.	
	22-2-18		HQ on 21st. New dug out at CAMBRIN proceeding. Tunnel at O.P. 1 CAMBRIN commenced. Men put on painting Hy Coy vehicles.	
	23-2-18		Dugout in MAISON ROUGE ALLEY suspended by order of C.E. I Corps. SAILLY POST excavation proceeded with.	

Army Form C. 2118.

WAR DIARY
INTELLIGENCE SUMMARY
(Erase heading not required).

ORIGINAL

Instructions regarding War Diaries and Intelligence Summaries are contained in F. S. Regs., Part II. and the Staff Manual respectively. Title pages will be prepared in manuscript.

Place	Date	Hour	Summary of Events and Information	Remarks and references to Appendices
LE QUESNOY	24-2-18		Strengthening of cellars at NOYELLES and 2 O.P's in FOSSE at NOEUX-LES-MINES completed. Notes taken of SALLY POST to facilitate connecting. Printing of boxes, vehicles proceeded with.	
	25-2-18		New dug-out with 3 entrances dug South of BEURY-BETHUNE Road. Working party arranged from 13th Labour Coy. Personnel as on 24th.	
	26-2-18		No 3 Section returned from detachment duty. Dug-out return to above, commenced. of half of any Labour Coy. was arranged immediately. Plumbing party at SALLY POST building main dug-out from the 2 tumbled entrances. Commenced a second O.P. in MAISON ROUGE ALLEY.	
	27-2-18		As on 26th. Note struck in new dug-out at BEURY ROAD and work stopped pending new instructions. Plumbing out and to form shafts at CAMBRIN dug-out.	
	28-2-18		Site of BEURY dug-out inspected by S.O.R.E. I Corps, & old site abandoned. Arrangements made for 170th Tunnelling Coy. to divert to Sap to site N. of BEURY-BETHUNE ROAD. Transport of materials to and especially of spoil at SALLY POST proving very great impediment to work. Erection of over-riders and shear-legs to expedite removal of spoil.	

Strength 1st Feby 1918
Officers   5
Other Ranks 204
Horses   70 (includes 13 in Mob. Vet. Sect.)

28th Feby 1918
Officers   6
O.R.   194
Horses   67.

Arrivals: 2/Lieut G. W. LORD from BASE. 10/7/18
Departures: 2/Lieut P. HALL to Hospital. 28/7/18

[signature]
Capt RE
D.O. 423rd Fd. Coy. R.E.

[signature]
Capt in the R.E.
M/C in the R.E.

A5834 Wt. W4973/M687 750,000 8/16 D. D. & L. Ltd. Forms/C.2118/13.

42nd Divisional Engineers.

428th FIELD COMPANY R. E.

MARCH 1918

Vol 14

WAR DIARY.
of
428 to (E. Lanc.) Fd. Coy. R.E.
from
1st to 31st. March. 1918.

(Volume 5).

Confidential
ORIGINAL

Army Form C. 2118.

WAR DIARY / INTELLIGENCE SUMMARY

ORIGINAL

(Erase heading not required.)

428TH (East Lancs) Field Coy. R.E.

Place	Date	Hour	Summary of Events and Information	Remarks and references to Appendices
LE QUESNOY	1/3/18		Bore hole made at site of proposed mined dugout N of the BEUVRY-BETHUNE Road — no water found at 14 feet, so decided to commence dug out to narrow gauge (Goman) employed at SAILLY POST for the day whilst about shift two cases pit hair. Shortage of labour at CAMBRIN affecting progress considerably. Started out new dugout at CAMBRIN O.P. Dugout now at front 26 feet of hard cover — opening out into chamber will commence on the 3rd. Night work on O.P. in MAISON ROUGE ALLEY. Painting of dug Vehicles provision of grocery boxes.	K.R
	2/3/18		As on 1st. Work commenced on D.H.Q. dugout N. of BEUVRY-BETHUNE Road. Concreting of tops of entrances to SAILLY POST shelter. Wire cable fixed up in working order at CAMBRIN DUGOUT. Excellent progress at O.P. in MAISON ROUGE ALLEY. Received Advance Cart from 126 M.G. Coy.	K.R
	3/3/18		New dugout off BEUVRY-BETHUNE Road proceeding. Inspected chimney at CIRCUS RELAY POST with a view to putting steps in it and a platform at top. Finished CAMBRIN DUGOUT OBSERVATION (O.P.) DUGOUT, and O.P. 2 in MAISON ROUGE ALLEY. SAILLY POST DUGOUT — Concreting proceeding and will finish in 2 or 3 days.	K.R
	4/3/18		Sappers employed on Yesterday. O.P. 2 still proceeding — now resetting the tunnel. Camouflage shell to the SAILLY POST DUGOUT.	K.R
	5/3/18		1 Officer, 2nd Lt. J.F.W.Welch, proceeded to join C.E. Fourth Army, leaving only 3 officers effective strength. Chamber in centre of the CAMBRIN DUGOUT almost excavated. O.P. in MAISON ROUGE ALLEY completed.	K.R
	6/3/18		At on 5th. Practice Shoot is at 8-45 p.m.	K.R
	7/3/18		As on 6th. Revetting at SAILLY POST finished. Banister cover and inner cover and section of tube commenced	O
	8/3/18		Tubo at SAILLY POST completed and bursts covered. Shell obtained from LABOURSE for job in hand by sanction of the chamber at CAMBRIN DUGOUT completed, and sinking commenced. Commenced putting in dogs and platform in chimney for O.P. off LA BASSEE ROAD. Sunk new dugout for 30 men at NOYELLES.	K.R
	9/3/18		As on 8th. Commenced new dugout off NOYELLES. Levelling ground and clearing site at SAILLY POST	K.R
	10/3/18		Cambrin O.P. and SAILLY POST dugouts and O.P. in Chimney near complete.	K.R
	11/3/18		Received plan from C.E. I Corps showing accommodation required in D.H.Q. dugout at BEUVRY. Work proceeding at CAMBRIN also NOYELLES Dugouts.	K.R
	12/3/18		As on 11th.	K.R
	13/3/18		As on 12th. Improvement of trestles etc at BEUVRY Dugout.	K.R
	14/3/18		Visited site of M.G. Shelter at BEUVRY Windmill. Shut water at NOYELLES — 22 feet average has sunk (12 feet chalk, 8 feet loam) do arrange to continue.	K.R
	15/3/18		Material to form road transported to Windmill.	K.R

Army Form C. 2118.

WAR DIARY
INTELLIGENCE SUMMARY
(Erase heading not required.)

Instructions regarding War Diaries and Intelligence Summaries are contained in F. S. Regs., Part II. and the Staff Manual respectively. Title pages will be prepared in manuscript.

Place	Date	Hour	Summary of Events and Information	Remarks and references to Appendices
LE QUESNOY	16-3-18		As on 15th. Work commenced on BEUVRY WINDMILL – cutting out for roofing joints. Assistance of 3 miners from 170 Tunnelling Coy. on BEUVRY DUGOUT. NOYELLES DUGOUT – turning of lock shaft to form dugout.	
	17-3-18		As on 16th.	
	18-3-18		2nd No chambers now finished at BEUVRY. Chiselling at WINDMILL proceeding.	
	19-3-18		Ground at BEUVRY very difficult to work. NOYELLES DUGOUT proceeding – forming centre chamber.	
	20-3-18		As on 18th. Neighbourhood of this dug heavily shelled; attached miners killed, 3 wounded, 10 sapper casualties. Shortage of gravel – using rank material from Corps Roads Office (at BEUVRY WINDMILL Nos.). Work at NOYELLES and BEUVRY Dugouts carried on with.	
	21.3.18		Lieut L.I. MARR arrived to replace Lieut J.F.W. WELCH. Centre dugout for 18 men at NOYELLES completed. 3 chambers at BEUVRY dugout completed. Company vehicles and teams being prepared for Divisional Transport Competition on 23rd inst.	
	22.3.18		As on 21st. Lieut OXLEY and 2 Limbers to LA BEUVRIERE to the shops – re called at 1 p.m. Company ordered to be prepared to move tomorrow – later definite orders to move received. Night shifts of sappers recalled. Vehicles packed. Spare baggage dispatched to Dumps at VAUDRICOURT with late sapper detailed to take charge.	
BUSNES	23.3.18		Company marched at 6.30am to BUSNES (less Transport which moved under separate orders and by road. Comp. (less Transport as above) entrained at BUSNES at 10 a.m., travelling via St POL, FRÉVENT, DOULLENS, HUMES to DOULLENS-ARRAS Rd. to ADINFER. Transport moved by Road & 30am via BRUAY, HOUDAIN, MAGNICOURT, reaching MONCHY BRETON. P. 3-30pm.	
ADINFER	24.3.18		Arrived ADINFER at about 1 a.m. and bivouaced the night where alighted. Day spent in finding water. Transport moved from MONCHY BRETON at 8am via TINQUES, AVESNES LE COMTE, BARLY, BAVINCOURT, POMMIER, BIENVILLERS-AU-BOIS where Lieut MARR met convoy and guided same to ADINFER arriving here about 12 midnight.	
	25.3.18.		1.30am. Comp. aroused and every rifle called for to cover 210th & 211th Brigades of artillery who were to go forward via DOUCHY and AYETTE. Few details (10 drivers 1 Corp. S.) and all Rifles left at ADINFER. Our Limbers with picks & shovels and 5 pack animals with spare S.A.A. accompanying the column fighting Rd. only carried. Guns took up position in valley west of COURCELLES and North	
West of COURCELLES			of ABLAINZEVILLE. Compy dug in on ridge about 500 yds. in advance of battery positions.	
South of LOG EAST WOOD			Artillery changed position to one South of LOG EAST WOOD at 2.30 pm and Comp. took up protective position in front, but had already not taken up new position when artillery returned to former	

A5834 Wt. W4973/M687 750,000 8/16 D. D. & L. Ltd. Forms/C.2118/13.

POST FORM C 2119

Army Form C. 2118.

WAR DIARY
or
INTELLIGENCE SUMMARY.

(Erase heading not required.)

Instructions regarding War Diaries and Intelligence Summaries are contained in F. S. Regs., Part II. and the Staff Manual respectively. Title pages will be prepared in manuscript.

Place	Date	Hour	Summary of Events and Information	Remarks and references to Appendices
WEST of COURCELLES (continued)	25.3.18		position along with Compy. a portion of this position being found to be occupied by detachment of M.G.C. moved again with batteries at 11 pm). Two sections rested in huts at ABLAINZEVILLE. (Lewthkor required for Lewis Gun Section), G.S. Limber + pack animals returned to Transport lines at ADINFER. Transport moved at 6 pm to POMMIER arriving towards midnight	B.Q.
	26.3.18		4am Two sections moved and proceeded to relieve remaining sections taking up position just South of LOG EAST WOOD and covering guns. 8am - after making 1 sections reformed further in Compy. in position. About 9am, a general retirement to immediate front began at once and artillery moved away along the road to ESSARTS. On departure of last gun Compy. retired in open order and reformed in BUCQUOY taking up front. position about 11am. Violent battle in Region of BUCQUOY proceeding. Orders received for Compy. to report to other field Companies in ESSARTS and to be directly under O.R.E. of Compy. moved at 10 pm + bivouaced in open field. Transport joined 26 Inf. Bde. Transport at ST. AMAND under orders of Col. CLIVE.	B.Q.
BUCQUOY.	27.3.18		Company handed over to 157 Inf. Bde. for running. Material obtained after much trouble and taken from ESSARTS to BUCQUOY Compy. marched to BUCQUOY and wired 800 x in front of 157 Inf. Bde. - A single lewis gun only being attempted. Compy. returned to ESSARTS at 4 am, 28th G.S. Wagon accompanied by 4 Sappers. proceeded to ADINFER to recover men's valises blankets etc.	B.Q.
ESSARTS.	28.3.18		Compy. occupying a series of trenches in rear of ESSARTS pending instructions from G.O.C. Compy. placed at disposal of G.O.C. 126th Inf. Bde. If G.C. to forward area to see our position. Compy. marched to line at 7pm. Guides from 5th Lanc. Regt. Occupied reserve trenches behind NEUVINZEVILLE. 2 O.R. Killed 1 O.R. (wounded to hospital) and 5 horses Killed, due to enemy shell fire. Transport moved to COUIN along with Brigade Transport.	
	29.3.18		Company holding reserve trenches with 1/5 E. Lancs Regt. Day spent mainly on improving trenches which were in a bad state owing to previous night's rain. Compy. relieved at 1am by 41st Division at 10.30pm and marched by sections to rear H.Q. arriving there at 1am 30th.	B.Q.
CONNECOURT WOOD.	30.3.18.		About 3am Compy. moved off to take up position in CONNECOURT WOOD for work under CRE in purple line, and after great difficulty found our destination (at old German lines) about 4am OC ordered by CRE to reconnoitre in 4 map square FOURRIERE and sit. Q(1.d.?)	(1.d.?)

A5834 Wt. W4973/M687 750.000 8/16 D.D.&L. Ltd. Forms/C.2118/13.

WAR DIARY
INTELLIGENCE SUMMARY.
(Erase heading not required.)

Army Form C. 2118.

Place	Date	Hour	Summary of Events and Information	Remarks and references to Appendices
GOMMECOURT WOOD	30.3.18 (continues)		points. Stores obtained and carried by infantry from FONQUEVILLERS (5 dumps made).	
	31.3.18		Company in dugouts in old German second line trenches. G.O.C. 125 Inf. Bde., O.C. and 2nd in command reconnoitred Purple Line, to wiring tonight from a point near GOMMECOURT WOOD to PIGEON WOOD with 126 Bde. Working Parties and transport of material arranged. Orders cancelled, no wiring, later it was decided that Company alone should carry out wire. This was done. Strength of Compy. on 31.3.18 :- 6 officers 201 other ranks, 66 animals.	

B. Roderick Major
O.C. 428th Fd. Coy. R.E.

428TH
(EAST LANCS.)
FIELD COMPANY, R.E.
Date 31.3.18

42nd Div.
IV.Corps.

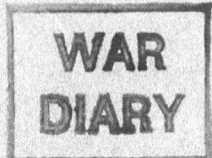

428th FIELD COMPANY, R.E.

A P R I L

1 9 1 8

WAR DIARY / INTELLIGENCE SUMMARY

Army Form C. 2118 — ORIGINAL

428th Field Company, R.E.

Place	Date	Hour	Summary of Events and Information	Remarks and references to Appendices
	1/4/18		4 Sections (about 114 strong) in the German 2nd line trenches at GOMMECOURT WOOD. Last nights wiring in front of purple line about 600x. Expected to relieve 2nd @ w/ RE for work on Red Line, but arrangements cancelled, and Company ordered to do line work with 12/5 Infy Bgde. Left GOMMECOURT WOOD for the line about 5 p.m. Each @ of 2 files. Cookers were C.S.M. & a few details. Left @ C.S.M. & a few details. Company. Was C.S.M. & a few details. Transport at COUIN — Kawies orders to move to-morrow to SOUASTRE.	/E.
	2/4/18		Company in the line. attacked by 115th E. Lancs. Regt. On night of 2/3rd Coy assisted by 160 Infantry dug an infantry new front Line. 350x in length, averaging 120x behind the old front line, which the two sides to the S.W. Corner of ABLAINZEVILLE Village. Worked from 9 p.m to 5.30 a.m. The 20 men wounded by enemy shell fire. COUIN at 8.30 a.m. by march route to SOUASTRE.	/E.
	3/4/18		On night of 3/4th Company with assistance of 160 Infantry & few Engrs Bn Garrison completed new front line commanded the previous night. In addition the posts of the front line no longer required for outposts were filled in.	/E.
	4/4/18		Infantry relief — no work by night except for salvage parties into obtained pickets & front boxes to improve stateboard.	/E.
	5/4/18		Rest by day. Work on Front line continues with assistance of a working party from 1/4th Ok Borderets Regt, who are in reserve, but told by 5th Infy Bde. Some wounded by enemy shell fire, and evacuated. One I.D. horse wounded.	/E.
	6/4/18		Work continues by day in the C.T. to ABLAINZEVILLE — 1 Section. 3 Sections RE and 130 Northumberland Fusiliers (Pioneers) made further efforts in the New Front line — widening and making Firestep. Very bad day — wet and ground in full condition. Two Blankets issued at Bn. HQ. at ESSARTS.	/E.
	7/4/18 8/4/18		Work from 4 p.m. - 9 p.m. on new Brigade Report Centre. Six work in front line. New Brigade Report Centre proceeded with. Two Blankets & 1 Box of Soup issued at Battn HQ. Company relieved by 457th Field Coy. R.E. (62nd Divn) Affiliated via MONCHY and BIENVILLERS to SOUASTRE, arriving at 10.30 p.m. They Bivouaced at midnight & PAS, arriving in billets at about 2 a.m. Than Transport arrived at 2.30 p.m. 4 PAS from SOUASTRE, arriving at destination 5 p.m.	/E.
	9/4/18		Men allowed to rest until 12 noon. Rest of day spent in cleaning up, bathing &c. No 1 Section returned to Sunken road near former position on the line to excavate 3 limbers from deep mud & returned with them at 11 p.m.	/E.
	10/4/18		Company at PAS in billets under 1 hours notice to move with 124th R.W. into position in 1st Line. Deficiencies of gum fits, clothing recognised also Coy equipment investigated. & hung rotis to move at 9 p.m., but nothing happened. The Division reconnoitred by 2 officers in neighbourhood of CHATEAU DE LA HAIE.	/E.

WAR DIARY or INTELLIGENCE SUMMARY

Army Form C. 2118.

(Erase heading not required.)

Instructions regarding War Diaries and Intelligence Summaries are contained in F.S. Regs., Part II. and the Staff Manual respectively. Title pages will be prepared in manuscript.

Place	Date	Hour	Summary of Events and Information	Remarks and references to Appendices
	11/4/18		Telegraphing up proceeded. Re-checking losses in Coy. equipment. 126th Inf. Bde. at 2:30 p.m. Coy. lines & fire details put through lachrymatory gas under D.G.O. from 4:30-5:30 p.m. Winning main to now to-morrow.	
	12/4/18		Company (less No.1 Section & Transport) moved to a position E. of COIGNEUX and bivouacked just W. of, and at the entry of work at J.16.d, for work on strong point at CHATEAU DE LA HAIE. N.C.O's reconnoitred road & track, digging done in afternoon.	
	13/4/18		Work on strong point at CHATEAU DE LA HAIE (V.6.a.6.6) proceeded. 1 load of wiring materials transport to job from HENU.	
	14/4/18		As on 13th. Further digging of small posts in existing trenches in CHATEAU DE LA HAIE. Wiring hedges (back of materials that went failed and hauled into position. Transport moved (on orders from 126th Bde.) from PAS to new lines near HENU at 9:53 a.m.	
	15/4/18		No work, as Coy. is to relieve 154th Field Coy. R.E. Advance party of Officers & N.C.O's to GOMMECOURT WOOD & wiring in front of GOMMECOURT LINE 9 Company arrived at 7:30 p.m. No.3 Section turned out for reconnaissance. Rain arrived at 3:30 p.m. 159 yards of fence. RUM TRENCH & GOMMECOURT LINE. Coy. moved to new GOIGNEUX – left HENU camp 5 p.m. arriving at new camp 6:30 p.m. for transport.	
	16/4/18		No. 1 Section changed over with No.2 Section, the proceeded to transport lines, three working under orders of C.R.E. 42nd Divn. No.1 Section wiring in front of RUM TRENCH. No. 2 Section taking & carrying timber for Coy. Blanket work from FONQUEVILLERS. New support line taped out & digging superintended by Coy. officer. 3 in a N.C.O's.	
	17/4/18		As on 16th. Digging by night on new Support Line. Fixing Gas Blankets at Bde. H.Q. Salvage timber from FONQUEVILLERS. Tramway from GOMMECOURT to BIEZ WOOD reconnoitred each day repair work heavily carried out. Coy. tent/tarpaulin superstructure of turtle wagon parked at ROSEL. G.L.D. mules drawn from PUGNEVILLERS.	
	18/4/18		2 New Strong Points dealt—one in N.W. corner of GOMMECOURT WOOD – one tall on SALMON TRENCH. Working parties arranged for each. Work all out & parties commenced work in afternoon. Wiring forward strong points by night. Large trolleying & carrying parties.	
	19/4/18		As on 18th. C.R.E. pointed out site of new locality around 4 dugouts on the FONQUEVILLERS – HEBUTERNE ROAD. Wiring & Trip-cutting of the 2 localities (SALMON & GOMMECOURT). Coy. H.Q. moved to old Bde. H.Q. dugouts in front of GOMMECOURT WOOD.	
	20/4/18		As on 19th. Work on GOMMECOURT Strong Point by day, and SALMON Strong Point by day & night.	
	21/4/18		As on 20th. Junior Trench ank: guard curtains for dugouts – chiefly at 3 Buff. H.Q.	
	22/4/18		Assistance given to infantry on HERRING TRENCH. 3 Platoon packs dug for Reserve Batt. in RUM SUPPORT. Provision of Notice Boards for Tunnelers, &c.	
	23/4/18		Work proceeding on JULIUS POINT and SALMON POINT. Salving material from JULIUS POINT trenches, fitting & filling in hold not required. Junk: Gas Blanket fitting at Bde. H.Q. & Batt. H.Q. continued. Stoppages & materials for wiring Buried Cable in tramway during last 2 days repaired carried out nightly on SALMON POINT.	

WAR DIARY or INTELLIGENCE SUMMARY

(Erase heading not required.)

Instructions regarding War Diaries and Intelligence Summaries are contained in F.S. Regs., Part II. and the Staff Manual respectively. Title pages will be prepared in manuscript.

Army Form C.2118.

Place	Date	Hour	Summary of Events and Information	Remarks and references to Appendices
	24/4/18		As on 23rd. Wiring materials extend. RUM SUPPORT deepened and trench made passable to Reserve Batt: HQ. Work at night installing stores to SALMON POINT running line. Clearing of HIGH ST continued. Preparation of 15000 sandbags of R.E. area N°2 Section from transport Road for work in forward Area. 2 I.D. horses killed, 2 wounded (one of which was eventually shot.) — Horse casualty due to enemy shell-fire.	/E.
	25/4/18		As on 24th. HIGH ST to be duckboarded at once, & 1 Coy N.F. (Pioneers) employed on this work. Brigade at HIGH ST. to indicate BIEZ SWITCH — commenced clearing trench with working party of 40. N°2 Section took over work in BIEZ SWITCH and SALMON POINT.	/E.
	26/4/18		Heavy of Arti:-Ger Trench M. Bomb M & G opened. Repairs to roads. Work in SALMON + JULIUS POINTS continued — filling in old trenches or batten place & completed. L.G positions sited on HIGH ST & BIEZ SWITCH. By night clearing and duckboarding HIGH ST to 428 Coy R.E. dump (Tramway) commenced. Material ordered to improve dug-outs near entrance to CHUB TR Batt HQ.	/E.
	27/4/18		As on 26th. Transport of stores by own transport from STAUREPAIRE.	/E.
	28/4/18		Work by day on HIGH ST. duckboarding. Tramway as on 27th. O.C. left temporary attachment to 126th Inf. Bde. HQ. leaving Capt. J. Entwistle in command. Pioneer Coy from H.Q. strength as 2.Bn. in Equipment — work commenced on BIEZ SWITCH. 1 Pioneer N killed down from 1/7th Manchester Regt.	/E.
	29/4/18		Work on JULIUS POINT by day & night — three "running" by dept to Coy of 1/7th K.F. (Pioneers) and 6 civvie Limbers. Party a subsequent of Emergency rally dumps. Party of 150 carrying during material to B. dump. Work on new entrance to Batt. H.Q. Dugout in SALMON TRENCH as Nassau Twp. into L.A. dump down from Ramparts 2013/4 VIII, owing to present Camp being in way of M.G. Range.	/E.
	30/4/18		Work bombarded to HIGH ST. but little work by day. Night party employed carrying wiring material forward to sunken road near Ridge with a fatigue to wiring BRASS and ASH trenches put an early finish. Company of Pioneers & 50 Infantry clearing & duckboarding HIGH ST by night, this C.T. being most useful.	/E.

Strength of Comp: 30.4.18 { 6 Officers
204 N.C.O
68 animals }

Casualties during month:— 5 O.R. wounded (4 H.F.P.)
8 O.R. sick

[signature]
Capt. R.E.
O.C. 428th Field Coy R.E.

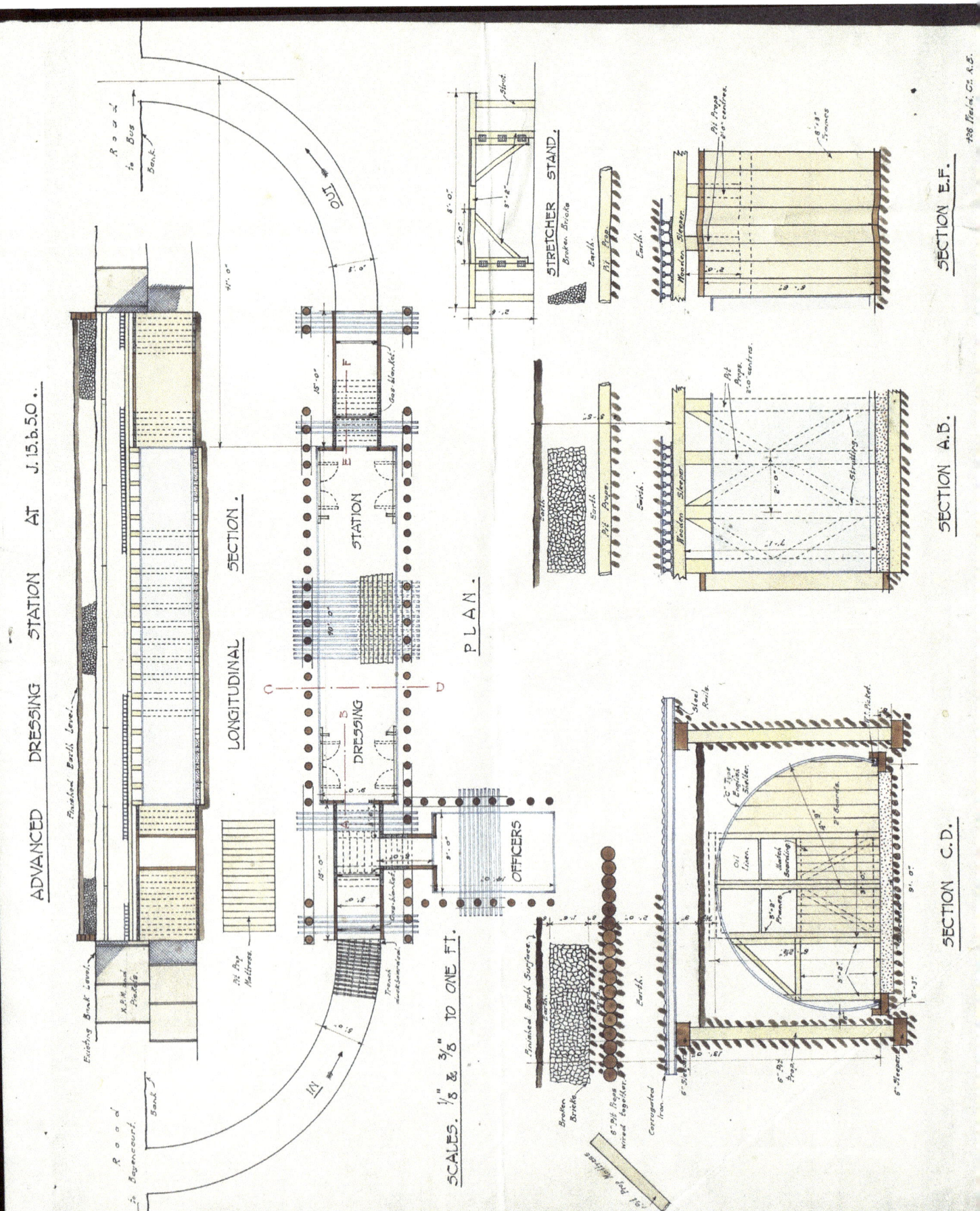

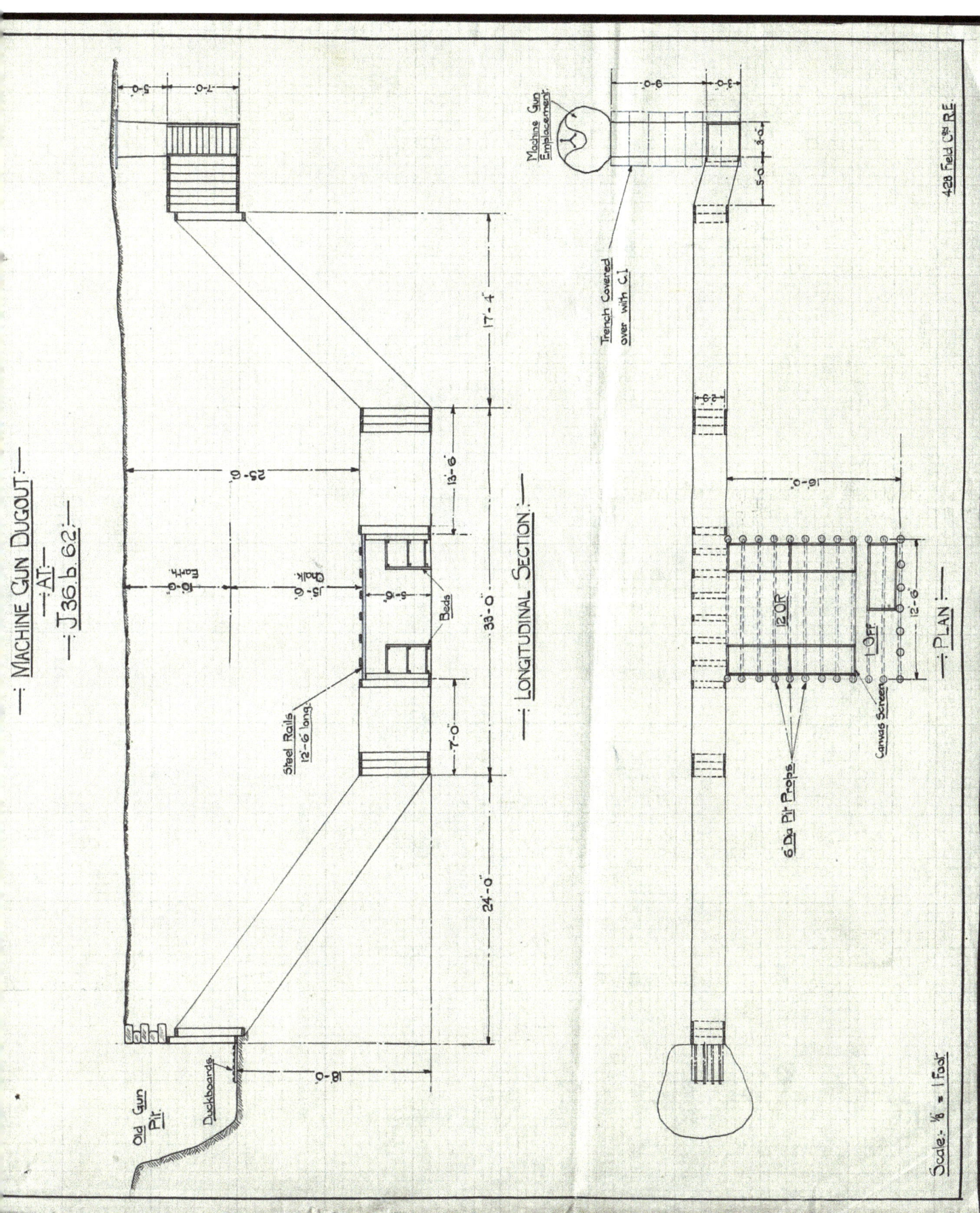

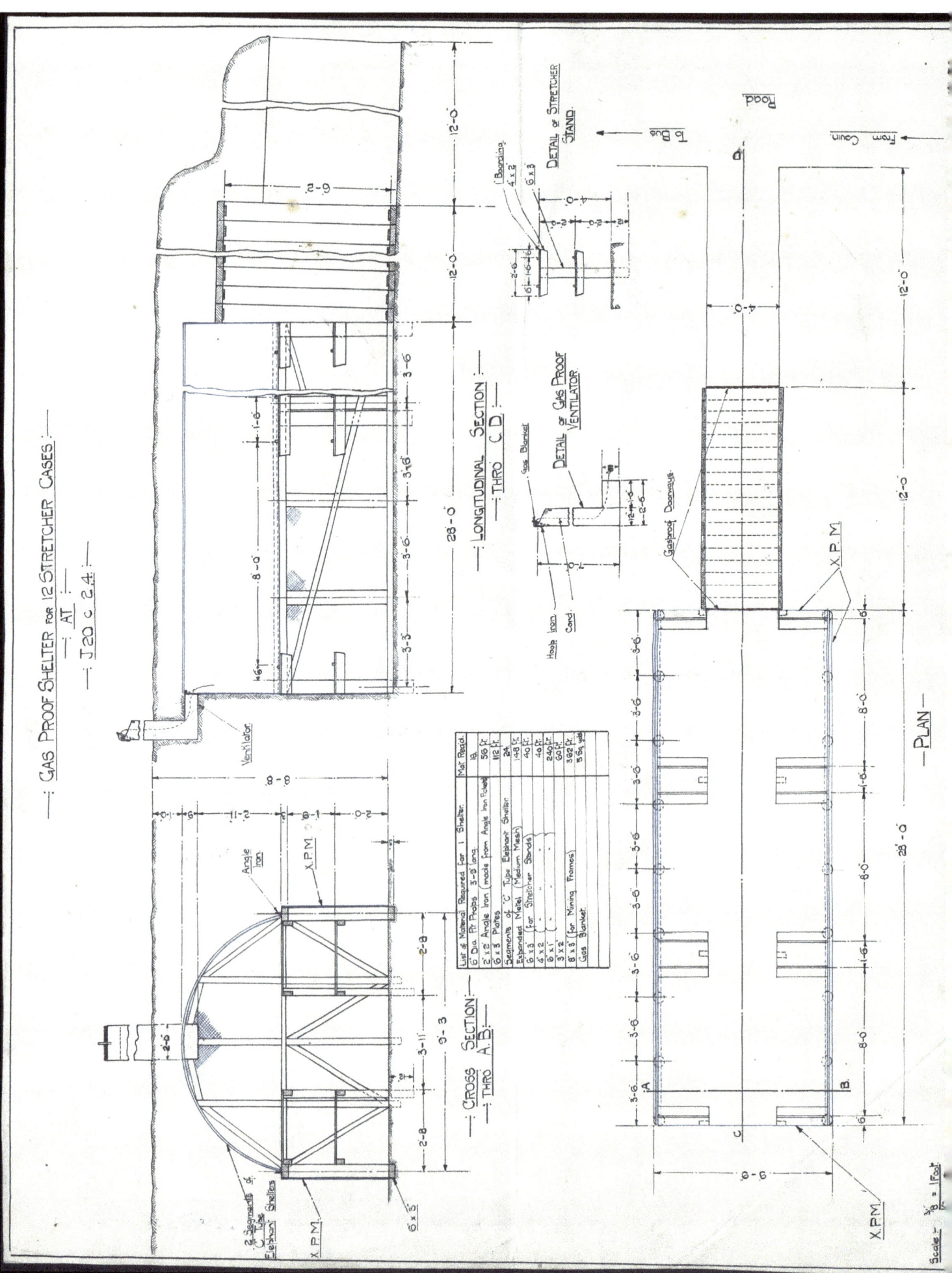

Army Form C. 2118.

WAR DIARY
INTELLIGENCE SUMMARY
(Erase heading not required.)

ORIGINAL Vol 16

Place	Date	Hour	Summary of Events and Information	Remarks and references to Appendices
			428th (E. Lancs.) Field Coy., R.E.	
	1.5.18		OC & 2nd in Command 423rd Field Coy. R.E. (54th Divr) called about midday concerning forthcoming taking over. Every effort made to expedite work on HIGH ST. Single completed almost up to WAAC ST. Orders received in afternoon to carry on with two strong points S. of FONQUEVILLERS. One at night was modified and all that had to be done was the wire in Bde. Hd.qrs. & M.G. Nest at E.27.c.6.0.	A/c.
	2.5.18		Work commenced on wiring S. of FONQUEVILLERS. Working party of 80 O.R. used for carrying wiring materials from Brigade Dump. No wiring parties at night owing to bright R.M.L.	A/c.
	3.5.18		Working parties obtained for work on JULIUS STRONG POINT and for wiring of S.P. South of FONQUEVILLERS which was practised on wire. Reconnaissance of CHUB ST. north of HIGH ST. made. Working parties at night commenced deepening CHUB ST. N of HIGH ST., BIEZ SWITCH, and deepening ASH TRENCH starting at the BASS end. Coy. Pioneers deepened OAK TRENCH.	A/c.
	4.5.18		Officer of 423rd Fd Coy. shown round all work by day on JULIUS POINT, and wiring of front line Blanketed at M.G.Coy. H.Q. wiring at E.27.c.6.0 also E.27.c.8.7. - Ground similar to that the Coy. to 429th Field Coy. R.E. Night parties (Pioneers) on CHUB TRENCH, BIEZ SWITCH, and ASH TRENCH. Parties of Sappers to supervise each party particulars of work off given the appointment book being over.	A/c.
	5.4.18		Work on wiring at E.27.c.6.0. & E.27.c.8.7. Handed over to 429th Field Coy. R.E. Sappers employed by night on improving pioneers nights work done on CHUB TR. & BIEZ SWITCH, and demolishing dugouts 11/13 & N.F. of M.G.Corps and improving new Battn H.Q. in SALMON TR. N of HIGH ST. One appr slightly wounded at Coy. R.E. Dump. Remained at duty, but was admitted to hospl. 2 days later. 50 Pioneers & Julius Point & 1 Coy on RUM SUPPORT cleaning & chipping At night Pioneers on OAK TRENCH - only that G.S. arrived. Or work raining. 70 steel sure. Rearrangement: 2 Companies on CHUB 1 Coy. on ASH, 1 Coy on BIEZ SWITCH, Remainder / Purple system 50 mm on JULIUS POINT, 1 Coy. on RYM SUPPORT. C.E II Corps wanted round front line of Purple system with representatives of 90719 & 91st Field Coys.	A/c.
	6.5.18		Company relieving the 423rd Field Coy at 8 P.M. and proceeded by march route to BOIS DE ST. PIERRE near PAS, reaching there at 11.50 P.M.	A/c.
	7.5.18		Coy employed on cleaning themselves up and erecting Latrines, Cookhouses re. 72 Pioneers under time of working to be sent on a mile march for 126th Infy. Bde. and various changes for RED LINE.	A/c.
	8.5.18		Work commenced on rifle ranges for 126th Infy. Bde. Camp improvements continued. The inspection of field and remainder front on Thursday.	A/c.

Army Form C. 2118.

ORIGINAL

WAR DIARY
INTELLIGENCE SUMMARY
(Erase heading not required.)

Instructions regarding War Diaries and Intelligence Summaries are contained in F.S. Regs., Part II and the Staff Manual respectively. Title pages will be prepared in manuscript.

Place	Date	Hour	Summary of Events and Information	Remarks and references to Appendices
	9.5.18		Training for Sections 2 and 4 continued, but interrupted by work, to practice the Battle positions Coy. to act as escort to 190th Bty R.F.A and to stand fast in camp until ordered to move out. Work on rifle ranges, hutting for 126th Inf. Bde. and camp improvements continued. In the evening a circus service was held. (C. of E.)	/C.
	10.5.18		Training continued from 8-15 a.m. to 12.30 p.m. In afternoon a football match was arranged between sections working on 9th inst. certain number of men taken off training to assist company mobiles.	/C.
	11.5.18		Paper chase held in afternoon.	/C.
	12.5.18		Church parade in morning for C.of E. Non-conformists, R.C. Remainder of day was a holiday for the men.	/C.
	13.5.18		Training continued, but No.1 Section was sent out on works on rifle range & for 126th Brigade instead of No. 3 which commenced to train.	/C.
	14.5.18		Sections 1 & 3 on firing on 25 and 50 yards ranges in the morning. Recruit and training in the afternoon.	/C.
	15.5.18		Training continued. Work as usual, but involved urgent hutting for an American battalion recently arrived.	/C.
	16.5.18		Sections 3 and 4 taken on to the assault course in the morning. No.1 Section continued on work on ranges for Brigade. No.2 Section employed on building 2 huts in PAS for American Army.	/C.
	17.5.18		Huts for WAMA completed. Work on range continued and training as usual. Firing on 25 yards improvised range in wood.	/C.
	18.5.18		Work on Baths at HENU commenced. Training for two sections only.	/C.
	19.5.18		Work on Baths at PAS commenced. Conference of O.C. Field Coys. at C.R.E.'s Office. One Section to be attached to 427th Field Coy. work to commence on 20th inst. Church Parade in evening.	/C.
	20.5.18		Only 1 section available for training, a composite section of backward men from other sections together with men who have not fired a sufficient number of rounds per week on actual range.	/C.
	21.5.18		No. 2 Section commenced work on manie dugouts - a few details filed on 200 range. Work on manie dugouts & baths at PAS and HENU continued.	/C.
	22.5.18		No 3 Section commenced new work on manie dugouts under 429th Field Coy. R.E. on a range at HENU (2 N.C.O's found for supervision only. Other work on or 21st.	/C.
	23.5.18		As on 22nd.	/C.
	24.5.18		As on 23rd.	/C.
	25.5.18		Work on baths continued. At HENU completed, and those at PAS workable pending completion of floor. Disinfestation room completed. 20 additional windmill targets for HENU Rifle range commenced. Liaison effected with L 295 Bde. R.F.A.	/C.

WAR DIARY or INTELLIGENCE SUMMARY

Army Form C. 2118.

ORIGINAL

Place	Date	Hour	Summary of Events and Information	Remarks and references to Appendices
	26.5.18		Preparation of diagrams to record N.C.O.'s men by Divisions. Commander in afternoon these worked in afternoon.	
	27.5.18		Reconnaissance made of work required on 2 new ramps in HENU valley. Work on disinfectors continued. 40 O.R. attended to Horse Lines of Coy. Vehicles.	
	28.5.18		Work personnel on ramps, minor dugouts. Minor repairs effected at PAS Bath.	
	29.5.18		continued to on 28th.	
	30.5.18		Lieut. W.B. Oxley leaves company for 5th Army troops, on appointment to Adjt. to C.R.E. 2nd Divt. Lt. T.E. Taylor & 4 N.C.O.'s proceed as delegate party to 502 & Field Coy. R.E. preparatory to taking over work from on 29th.	
	31.5.18		G.R.E. and Dvt. Quartermaster inspect transport lines. Commenced work on erection of 3 huts at Commerce Camp at HALLOY. Erection of ramps at PAS Bath. Work on minor dugouts continued.	

Strength of Coy. 31.5.18.
Officers 6.
O.R. 206.
Animals 72.

Casualties during month.
14 O.R. Sick.
1 O.R. Wounded.
2 O.R. Killed.   } 18 O.R.
1 O.R. died of wounds.

16 O.R. Reinforcements joined Coy.

Animals evacuated.
8 " " drawn (?)
Remounts.

Signed [signature]
Major
O.C. 488th Fd. Coy. R.E.

Army Form C. 2118.

WAR DIARY
or
INTELLIGENCE SUMMARY.
(Erase heading not required.)

428TH (East Lancs) FIELD COY. R.E.

Place	Date	Hour	Summary of Events and Information	Remarks and references to Appendices
PAS.	1.6.18		Company engaged in erection of Dining Mess Hut for Div. Rest Camp at HALLOY. — Erection of 2 Jerney Huts. Sgt with Cagli Boiler Hut for Div. Baths. Work proceeding on Shelter Dugout for D.H.Q. on the PAS- COUN Road S.I.A. 4.9. Advance party of 1 officer and 4 N.C.O's sent to take over work from Right by 552D Field Coy R.E., retrieves and ammunition of orders for Div. relief, a Vincennes party was not sent.	ƒ.
	2.6.18		As on 1st.	ƒ.
	3.6.18		1 Officer and 4 N.C.O's sent to billets of 2nd N.Z.E. to take over work and demolition work in the camp of Right Div. Sector. 1 Officer took over Company from R.E. Base Depot. Work as on 1st inst. II Lieut. K.H. READ. R.E.	ƒ.
	4.6.18		Orders received that whilst taking over work from 2nd Fd Coy. N.Z.E. the camp of the 154 R Fd. Coy. R.E. was also to be taken over by advance party.	ƒ.
	5.6.18		Starting at HALLOY completed. 1 Officer and 4 O.R. sent as advance party to BUS to take over camp from 154 Fd. Coy. (37 Din) who were moving out of the area before Coy moved in.	ƒ.
	6.6.18		Work as above continued until 2 p.m. Remainder of day spent in cleaning up & washing Coy. vehicle. &c.	ƒ.
	7.6.18		Company moved to BUS WOODS. The Advance Section & Transport moving via COUIN to a new site off the BUS. LOUVENCOURT ROAD an officer of the 179 R Tunnelling Coy. RE attacked for duty to advise on dugout construction.	ƒ.
BUS.	8.6.18		Company engaged on work as follows:— Reconnaissance of CATACOMBS in BUS Chateau grounds. Excavation being treated as visit a view to finding further galleries &t a lower depth. The present workings are reached by three subterranean shafts, which are thought to have been former air vents. News from the work in BUS Chateau. Work on dugout (mined) work at Chambers and surface observation post at FORT BERTHA. Shaft dugout work at J.36. d.3.6.EP. No 4 Section detached on retrenchment R.A. R.E. work whilst the company is in reserve, their work consisting chiefly of supervision of working parties, being attained from the Arkely Brigades concerned	ƒ.

WAR DIARY or INTELLIGENCE SUMMARY

Army Form C. 2118.

(Erase heading not required.)

Place	Date	Hour	Summary of Events and Information	Remarks and references to Appendices
	9.6.18		Work as usual. Small detachment sent to HALLOY to erect further munition huts. Work commenced on the erection of 5 C.S. Shelters by surface labour, personnel S.N.Q. Dugout at I.23. central, & working party of 20 O.R. from 2/NZ Division being assembled. Flooring of rooms in Bus Chateau completed, with shelving to ground floor and ceiling, & on A.P.	
	10.6.18			
	11.6.18		Work as detailed on 8th inst. pursuing. Lack of working parties for urgent proving work, e.g. work in R.E. Saloon Beginning rifle, for 2 waiting rooms at LOUVENCOURT Railway Station made these late in the field. In the Pit case, 100 cubic portions of work covered in, and vacant offices in the others, and shelters caving. Work re completion of BUS CATACOMBS stopped, pending a decision being given as to their making up cost of earthworks, the overhead covering being 23 ft minimum. Working party of 10 R.A.M.C. engaged on Ruts at LOUVENCOURT Station.	
	12.6.18	"		
	13.6.18		At 9.12th, 18 Alpine Hero reptd LOWE system with all spring in BUS Work forth was 1 /40 Bttn. M.G.C. An average of 10 men per day now being moved there with T.R.B.	
	14.6.18		Work continued as above. Shortage of timber interfering with progress on putting sub for Loading Road into complete a new A.R.P closure in I.24.d. This indent will be dep., in length when complete. Arrangements made with Staff Capt. R.E. for working parts of 20 O.R. all materials. Re. dealings, to be obtained from standard R.E. DUMP (ELSTON) in forward areas.	
	15.6.18		Hutting at HALLOY completed and detachment of 8 O.R. returned to Company. Work in Brigade Send No 16 handed over to R.A.R.D. officer, from to-day S.O.R. attached Government repts mess hand-over duty on the 1 BUS. BERTRANCOURT TFend. Sewell man of the above Company continues duty on a form of influenza which appears to contain other Company.	
	16.6.18		Above referred to hand over wrote on M.G. dugt. Arril No.24 to Major Butt, in view of work on reproc and maintenance of BEER, RUM, CANTERBURY and CORP trenches; position effected and work, req his R.E. and unit arranged so as to fit in with his scheme. Position ? C.S. Shelters and H.Q. embodying lines, covering and work proposed for FORT HEROD defence.	
	17.6.18		It had been considered necessary to double alternate segments of the system in view of the great weight of infantry to be employed and to avoid infantry shutting up Coys of infantry employed on BEER and CORP trenches, starting at LOUVENCOURT District, completing at LM.	

Army Form C. 2118.

ORIGINAL

WAR DIARY
or
INTELLIGENCE SUMMARY.
(Erase heading not required.)

Instructions regarding War Diaries and Intelligence Summaries are contained in F. S. Regs., Part II. and the Staff Manual respectively. Title pages will be prepared in manuscript.

Place	Date	Hour	Summary of Events and Information	Remarks and references to Appendices
	18.6.18		Ap. on 17th. Small party of support of transport lines erecting walls for protection of animals.	
	19.6.18		The double apron fence having been considered unsuitable for infantry in high wire, Design still as adopted was received to instruct infantry given to 1 Coy of Reserve Battn. daily.	
	20.6.18		Work as on 17th. Reconnaissance made with O.C. Field Ambce. for new A.D.S. site chosen just north of the BUS-BAYENCOURT Road. Snow-country hut in vicinity which could make it suitable & erected.	
	21.6.18		Working parties of 60. R.A.M.C. (in 2 shifts) on excavation for new A.D.S. which is to be a 40' C.S. Shelter with two open approaches, supported by 2 stronly braced centre frames 2 feet thick with overhang timber, mattress ? 8" to 10" ? which together with outer skin finally covered by 6" earth. The officer attached from the 17th Immobile By R.E. returned to his unit.	
	22.6.18		Work as on 21st inst. Towards of By Stumpess from works through inquiries to him men reached working parties to D.A.D.L. (I ? 3 Cent.) what had been formed by M.G. Battalion now replaced by infantry.	
	23.6.18		Infantry parties for BEER and CANTERBURY shelters unavailable for 23rd inst. owing to Inf. Brigade itself at work or entraining, draining & continuing to cupers.	
	24.6.18		Reconnoitred out plans prepared for two Gas Purf. Col room Dugouts for reception of Shelter cases from main Dressing Stations in case of Gas attack. Work continued on D.A.P. Shelter which are now complete with the exception of Gas-proofing. Caning Road 12' wide continued. Short sapping being made to level up the hollow between the Relieve pillows. Excavation for new A.D.S. continued & shelter partly erected.	
	25.6.18		Work as on 24th. In addition work was recommenced on M.G. Dugout, serial No. 24 in V.36 A.16 or of M.G.C. in 2 shifts being employed. 2 Coys of Infantry again available for BEER and CANTERBURY Shelters.	
	26.6.18		Civil Transport employed daily in transporting also R.E. material from stations forward dumps for BEER and for A.D.S. As on 25th inst.	

Army Form C. 2118.

WAR DIARY
or
INTELLIGENCE SUMMARY.
(Erase heading not required.)

ORIGINAL

Instructions regarding War Diaries and Intelligence Summaries are contained in F. S. Regs., Part II. and the Staff Manual respectively. Title pages will be prepared in manuscript.

Place	Date	Hour	Summary of Events and Information	Remarks and references to Appendices
	27.6.18		At no. 25 unit. Corduroy Road in I.24.d. completed, and work commenced on provision of bunks for 20 OR at Hilltop Bde. H.Q. Dugout at I.23.a.7.2. Shelters for Dr.s &t I.23 central completed. Carpentry of the sleep dug out & provision of light furniture handed over to 3 sections by M2E on inspection from C.R.E. 42nd Divn. Other wgrs on yesterday.	
	28.6.18		Work as on 28th. Enquiry for first shelter (gun emplt) for 12 shelters each 2 L205. Proceeding. A party of 12 R.A.M.C. according to A.D.S. at no M.G. Engrs to continue. Site reconnoitred in I.30.b.75.60 for two M.G. Pill-boxes, each to contain 2 Vickers gun personnel.	
	29.6.18		Working on 29th including transport of materials by any night of bricks from dump to site of A.D.S. and shelters from dump No 24 connected with sunken lane in COURCELLES top up entrance from dug out. M.G. Emplacement prepared for use, using English mounting. Mould for proper M.G. Emplacement to be commenced forthwith. Work on the two pill-boxes arranged to be	
	30.6.18		Casualties during month :- To hospital (sick) 20. Rejoined Compy from hospital } 10. Reinforcement received. 6. Ground Strength :- 7 officers (includes 1 in hospital) 202 OR (-11-6")	

A5834 Wt. W4972/M687 750,000 8/16 D. D. & L. Ltd. Forms/C.2118/13.

[Stamp: 428TH (EAST LANCS.) FIELD COMPANY, R.E. No. ____ Date 30.6.18]

[Signature]
Major
O.C. 428th Fd. Coy. R.E.

WAR DIARY

Army Form C. 2118.

~~INTELLIGENCE SUMMARY~~
(Erase heading not required.)

ORIGINAL Vol/8

428TH (East Lancs) FIELD COY. R.E.

Place	Date	Hour	Summary of Events and Information	Remarks and references to Appendices
SHEET 57.D. Coy H.Q. & No 1. 1/4 Section at BUS-LES-ARTOIS (J.20.b.5.0) Tspt Lines at J.31.b.2.8 (on BUS- LOUVENCOURT ROAD)	1.7.18		Company in reserve, 1 Section (No 4) being engaged on R.A.R.E. work (chiefly supervision of construction of) and improvements and repairs to tunnelled dugouts) remaining elections of M.G. Positions & on rearward area, in lieu of [illegible] & general reserve work in hand at date:- Improvements to CANTERBURY AVE. from R.25.a.70.25 to R.25.d.3.8. - Erection of 2 Barnwall Shelters for Stretcher cases at J.20.c.15.20. - New A.D.S. at J.15.b.5.0. - M.G. (Vermelles) Dugout at J.36.a1.33.83, - Concrete Pill Box with 2 M.G. Loopholes at J.30.b.7.6. - Bunking to Dugout R.23.a.7.2. - Patrolling, reconditioning of tracks. - 2 Supply & mine frames at J.20.c.11. - Construction of muck walls for protection of animals at tpt [?]. - Excavation for geo[?] & shelters and ADS continued. CANTERBURY AVE. 280' completed and duckboarded. Concrete M.G. at Coy H.Q. approx ½ finished & completed in dugout at J.23.a.7.2. Erecting moulds of ICPs and of M.G.Batts. Patrolling tracks & fixing notice boards sliding parts for transport carrying materials for P.Bs. Box by night.	J.G.
	2.7.18		Work as on 1st. Cleaning site for M.G. Pill Boxes. Bunking of Dugout at J.23.a.7.2 held up for lack of material. Work on CANTERBURY AVE ceased.	J.G.
	3.7.18		As on 2D. Arranged for W.P's from 125th Inf Bde for work on FORT BERTHA CRIMEA LOCALITY, wiring in the Purple Reserve to RAM.C. Transport by day bringing materials to A.D.S. 3.G.S. Waggon by night with stores for Pill Box. Train G.S. Waggon later with water tank to convey water to Concreting at M.G.Pill Box. Part of A.D.S. 40' shutter completed so far as Engr H.Q. 2 the part earthing shaft adopted to 90th. Bunking of frame mining sets for first F.A.B. prop shelter at J.20.c.15.20. 1 officer (Capt AN. WALKER) to Paris on short leave.)	J.G.
	4.7.18		New work commenced with W.P working parties as follows:- FORT BERTHA (2 Platoons) CRIMEA LOCALITY (2 Platoons) wiring in front of purple Picture (1 Company) Other work continued. Rails, posts, and barbed in transported nightly from advanced dump (EUSTON). Reid TE.Taylor proceeds to ABBEVILLE for Veterinary course. Only OC & subalterns left for general work through shortage of officers. much felt. Sergt KINLEY gains special mention for work at army musketry course.	J.G.
	5.7.18		Work continuing as previous day. 150' Standard high wire (10' wide) was erected from J.34.6.20 working N. The work was preventing the 57 ½ Bn Brit. R.E. Staff falling previously at M.G. Box Dugout No.24 now complete & handed over for occupation to 3rd. Excavation for M.G. Pill Box continued & digging in watersupply trench. 1 Sapper & 20 Infty preparing Dugouts near Batt. R.E. Dump in area. A new storage point listed in BEAUSSART SWITCH terminated. 12 OR North Fus (A) attached, to relieve sappers being much needed.	J.G.

WAR DIARY
or
INTELLIGENCE SUMMARY.
(Erase heading not required.)

Army Form C. 2118.

Instructions regarding War Diaries and Intelligence Summaries are contained in F. S. Regs., Part II. and the Staff Manual respectively. Title pages will be prepared in manuscript.

Place	Date	Hour	Summary of Events and Information	Remarks and references to Appendices
	6.7.18		FORT BERTHA — 200' trench completed to full height. CRIMEA LOCALITY — Continued widening, deepening, firestepping M.G. Pill Box. Excavation relieving for floor footings 90% complete. Collecting fuel from old camps and packing A.D.S. — Roof complete has dug in to. Shelter corner. Officers shelter erects rifle frames complete. Approach trench commenced. Painting, littering signboards etc. Purple Splinter, Purple Splinter etc. Preparing Kms etc. M.G. Dugout, Lew. posn Shelter etc. continued. Coy. draughtsmen locating dugouts on Bn. area & preparing schedule of same.	✓
	7.7.18		Work started out two localities off BEAUSSART SWITCH — Commenced firestepping & deepening forward slopes in locality No. 1, also commenced work continued in Shang Pointe. Banking brink, & excavation for flow springing & concreting same almost 75%. Collecting about 450 fts to firm. R.E. dump complete. Method at O.P.'s in camps. Distributed annually bags to A.D.S. 50% complete. Erection of mining frames to extreme & roofs complete. 32 Coy. Infantry at work today W.P.d approved & employed on locality.	✓
	8.7.18		FORT BERTHA — Extension of BESS AVENUE to Pot B3 completed and firesteeped. Collecting wiring captured on old CRIMEA AVE continued. Clearing foregourd and wiring pickets for wire. CRIMEA LOCALITY — Firestepping of CRIMEA AVE. Locality No. 1 (P.6.9.15) Beatty's Platoon first morning out & clearing in the night until 8am. Locality No. 2 — 20 infantry BEAUSSART SWITCH — Locality No. 1 (P.6.9.15) Beatty's Platoon first morning out & clearing in the night until 8am. forming small dumps. W.P arrived without tools. They were improved with shovels. Substantial underwalks also remained. Work previous on trench exit M.G. Pill Box — Continuing to fronting completion. Cleaning floor & etc. Cleaning dcnos, simpley except my entrance to Purple Splinter made within minutes. A.D.S — Officers Shelter. Roof autumn, erecting 62 Zin Notice Boards at various spots. 62 Zin Notice Boards for Purple Splinter made within minutes. Erected Officers Shelter. Roof autumn, preceding 15 places in Pavilion at various spots. 70 Knife Rests prepared to date and 15 places in Pavilion at various spots. 32RE's wire assemble in event of an Bristol undergoings in L20.a found by Asst. 32nd R.E. Pat Kin Coy, where 32RE's wire assemble in event of an alarm.	✓
	9.7.18		Work as yesterday but that nothing was done at FORT BERTHA. W.P. being diverted to BEAUSSART SWITCH LOCALITY NO.1, Party of 12 Suppers who travelled 3 Nissen huts at present D.H.Q & these huts were transported to site of new DHQ at L23 Central, preparing to re-erect there tomorrow. Qr Master W.P arranges for erection Huts was tried with success on ground. Corps which militia will feel of fine at localities.	✓
	10.7.18		Party of 12 Suppers, 12 NF(P), 2-20 infy erected 3 Nissen huts at new D.H.Q. between 6:30 am. & 7:30 pm. Officers took at new q.M.S hut W.Pd worked only till noon owing to holes. Beyond relief.	✓
	11.7.18		Improvements to trenches, wiring etc examined M.G. Good progress at M.G. Pill Box. Carpentry to at CRIMEA LOCALITY. Improved at Shang Pointe continued. Commenced M.G. Good progress at M.G. Pill Box. Carpentry to shelters employed complete, any walk commenced at new D.H.Q. making floor, cookhouse etc. Huts erected completely. Commenced improvement made and 35 transported to site where reflect floors to commenced work on Pill Box, dug 85 knife rests made and 35 transported to site where reflect floors to date 950 large boards found at R.E. Dump also created. 92 Notice boards for truste & panellet erected to	✓

A5834 Wt. W4973/M687 750,000 8/16 D. D. & L. Ltd. Forms/C.2118/13.

Army Form C. 2118.

WAR DIARY
or
INTELLIGENCE SUMMARY.
(Erase heading not required.)

Instructions regarding War Diaries and Intelligence Summaries are contained in F. S. Regs, Part II. and the Staff Manual respectively. Title pages will be prepared in manuscript.

Place	Date	Hour	Summary of Events and Information	Remarks and references to Appendices
	12.7.18		All gates cased up as yesterday. Excellent progress made at HQ (I 23 central). Third day chalk for shuttering will be complete. The pump shute will be partly erected with BEAUSSART SWITCH to BERT AVENUE 50% completed. Bike work proceeding satisfactorily. 12 extra officers during the week. T.E. Taylor returned Coy from Vetheuil any course at Abbeville.	
	13.7.18		Work on FORT BERTHA localities canals running BEAUSSART SWITCH to BERT AVE. 100% complete. Work on other Site wall of M.G. Pill Box - work on BEAUSSART SWITCH LOCALITY N°1 to be dismantled. First progress made on work at A.D.S. and it is now possible to use same by completing topics. 9 huts week fixed at stage in use and airplanes painted and erected as necessary for R.A. PURPLE SYSTEM. N°4 Station Switched the ampleos opening airplant construction for R.A. 1 H.P. admitted to 18th M.V.S.	
	14.7.18		M.G. Tim Dugout (Serial N°24) – duckboards kept entrance manways improved – the whole dugout was completed working parties from 137th Inf. Bde. rearranged during 2 platoons work again on BEAUSSART SWITCH N°2. Principal work on A.D.S. approaching completion. N°1 Gas proof shelter at J15 c.15.20 now completed. 200 yd (Broad Complex) employed on construction of new road to D.H.Q. at I23 central. Driver employed on shuttering other work. other works now in N°39 SHAFT HAVRE Capt. A.N. WALKER demitted to hospital while on leave.	
	15.7.18		At on 14th. Right Ride. moved into new HQ at FORT BERTHA on which the Coy. is busily engaged.	
	16.7.18		As yesterday. Work on road at I23 central proceeding. 8 G.S. Wagons carting chalks for foundation 2 Buster Lorries collecting road metal from Stone Dump at AUTHIE. Work commenced on BRETT HQ at J30 d.6.1 - gas proofing and finishing Inf. parties on localities as usual. M.G. Pill Box advanced up to height of 3ft.	
	17.7.18		Wiring proceeding at all the localities except FORT BERTHA. Excavation for 2" Gas-proof Shelter at J.20.C.15.20. carried on with. 30% chalk foundation laid for road at I23 central. Other work on previous day.	
	18.7.18		All hutting at D.H.Q. (I23 central) completed. 33 Rings Reads & 17 gas blankets fixed during this week. All work proceeding favourably.	
	19.7.18		No work on FORT BERTHA & CRAMER localities, owing to wire-Bise netting, including erection of shelter shutters. Work on BEAUSSART SWITCH LOCALITIES N° 1 & 2 Carried on with. Other work on hand proceeded with.	

Army Form C. 2118.

WAR DIARY
or
INTELLIGENCE SUMMARY.
(Erase heading not required.)

Instructions regarding War Diaries and Intelligence Summaries are contained in F.S. Regs., Part II. and the Staff Manual respectively. Title pages will be prepared in manuscript.

Place	Date	Hour	Summary of Events and Information	Remarks and references to Appendices
	20.7.18		Concreting roof of M.G. Pill Box. Preparing shuttering for O.P. on roof, and site for a second pill-box being prepared. BEAUSSART SWITCH Locality N°1 (was known as ORCHARD POINT) completed - gunnion putting in trench shelters. N°2 (known as CUTTING POINT) work on wiring, digging, revetting shelters (2 to date) carried on with. A.D.S. dug-out, trench knife course revetting to entrance completed. Excavation for, & concreting of, foundations for MOIR PILL BOX at J.23.c.95.80 completed.	
	21.7.18		Gunnion at ORCHARD POINT assisted to put in trench Shelters. Other work preparing. Work on MUSTARD POINT & SHRINE POINT WEST (consisting of improving existing trenches running through), & commenced on erection of 2 Type shelters on a sunken [?] by R.E. taken over from 42nd Div[?] Coy R.E. Removal of Belle Buffs in purple system.	
	22.7.18		All work carried on as usual. MOIR Pill Box in course of erection. It was found that with a junior N.C.O. to supervise the erection took 108 manhours [?] exclusive of concrete to roof, & more than [?] a junior officer.	
	23.7.18		MOIR PILL Box at J.23.c.95.80 completed. Bad weather conditions - Rag [?] unprogress train work being carried out in localities. Other work progresses favorably.	
	24.7.18		Commenced erecting O.P. to Pill Box at J.30.b.76 - concreting of roof to this Pill Box nearing completion. Filing at FORT BERTHA, CRIMEA, and CUTTING POINT progresses with digging through MUSTARD POINT and SHRINE WEST Localities, & approx 4 bays of Rev[?] Bays. erecting gang of Type shelters within this Area.	
	25.7.18		As on 24th. A tenton roller of trench [?] Corps to all new road at I.23 central. In [?] am attempt at being made to put 150 tons of metal over it. Their is proving a [?] proposition.	
	26.7.18		N°1 Pill Box Completed, employees handed over to Sanfield mountings & into platforms. Adjusting shaft chamber & official chamber at A.D.S. Provided boiler at BERTRANCOURT Sike repaired.	
	27.7.18		In accordance with warning order that O.C. refusing end of 57 KCns shown agreed all work in hand. A.D.S. Completed with changing at [?] the one & the ensection of 3 hour Company at Bus Chateau the auto which [?] magically taken on in hand. Them pulling removed to 3 dump, on labour available have been to keep 3 working continually. The order of preceding of work in Locality is as follows: Dipping of timbers to be the absolute minimum return drainage sumps, morning.	

A5834 Wt. W4973/M687 750,000 8/16 D.D. & L. Ltd. Forms/C.2118/13.

WAR DIARY
or
INTELLIGENCE SUMMARY.
(Erase heading not required.)

Army Form C. 2118.

Place	Date	Hour	Summary of Events and Information	Remarks and references to Appendices
	27.7.18	contd	...finally. Construction of further Burst Construction 8'x4' infant shelters to prevent rainwater from entering dug-outs & within the localities. Surface improvements at Ryd 13 being continued.	
	28.7.18		No.1 Coy R.E. Batt: Stn provided ammunition store provided. Altelier etc above. completed. Water for RAMC Arrangements made for RAMC to provide working parties on improvements to the Bus-BAYENCOURT to Ads. supplies in and report and slip rails to the trench. Work completed. ADS. Lieut R.A. Baldwin arrived from No.B.D. on other work in progress.	
	29.7.18		2nd Battalion of Kens.Fus. visited to ensure continuity of labour on boundaries of 11-12 PDR BATT position within company area. Work continued at the connectry of 11/2 PDR BATT position will be disposed with. They large mod RPM merits of standing likely to be received by BERTHA MUSTARD SHRINE & W localities. Execution of (out 13) Western Belts completed. By 90 OR AD MUSTARD POINT begun. Execution of (out 13) Eastern debouchy cancelled by 57th East debouchy cancelled.	
	30.7.18		Work continued as yesterday. During the ADS. being completed before the Bus. BAYENCOURT road. improvements are finished, a party of 30 RAMC arranged for to dig drains also permanent addit to bring the Coy to this work as soon as the DHA and at I.23 Cythel is completed. 10-ton lorry changed to recon wells in COURCELLES and COLINCAMPS with a view to provision of power driven pumps. Inspection of bath at VAUCHELLES with a view to provision of similar installation at BERTRANCOURT. 35 OR 17G N.F. (P) arranged for to expedite work on SHRINE POINT RAT locally. Road party of I.23 Central unexpect from working strength of 85. OR no other work must be completed before further rain.	
	31.7.18		Reconnaissance of well at COURCELLES & COLINCAMPS. Trench hut 35'x18' commenced for Reserve Batt. K.R.R. Bn. (WR. in locality) Provided as yesterday. exhausted from Rt Bn. the two (which will subsequently provide the garrison) providing additional parties for work on trench shelters, cook-houses, and water storage general.	
			Plans attached:— 1. Machine Gun Dugout and Pop-up erected at J.36.b.6.2. (South of COLINCAMPS) 2. Gas proof shelter for 12 shuttered cases at J.20.c.2.7. (BUS-lles - ARTOIS) 3. Advanced Dressing Station at J.15.b.5.0. (N. of the BUS-BAYENCOURT Road) Strength of Company on 31.7.18:— Officers 7 O.R. 204. Attached 72. (Casualties during month caused by sickness only.)	

Major

WAR DIARY
INTELLIGENCE SUMMARY
428th FIELD COY. R.E.

Army Form C. 2118.

Sheet 1

Place	Date	Hour	Summary of Events and Information	Remarks and references to Appendices
Coy HQ & Nos. 4 & 3 Sections at J20.b.50 (Bus aux Artois Woods)	1-8-18		Company engaged on :- digging & improving trenches running to at MUSTARD, SHRINE EAST & SHRINE WEST Localities, construction of dugouts concrete M.G. Pill-Box at J.30.b.7.7, construction of road at J.23 central, improvement of road in J.15d. (approach to new A.D.S.), erection of 3 Nissen Huts at Chateau, Bus, erection of shelters, gas proof for officers & orderlies at Bus. HQ. J35.c.7.2. Shelters for Battn HQ. at J.31.b.2.6., for Coy HQ. at J.23.b.9.2. Gas proofing plumbing for garrisons at MUSTARD SHRINE EAST, SHRINE WEST, ORCHARD & CUTTING POINTS. HQ. P.6.6.3.1. 1 Section (No.4) engaged on R.A. RR. work, consisting construction of dugouts &c. Party employed daily cleaning & repairing Ly. which is improving. Horse Lines OC Coy (Major J. Entwistle) left to proceed on leave to UK, Capt CF.T. Jones (429th Fd. Coy RE) assumed command during his absence.	/c
M.M. Section Transport J31.b.2.8 (nr Bus, Louvencourt Rd)				
Sheets 57c & 57d	2.8.18		Commenced work at Baths COURCELLES-AU-BOIS, installing power pump, storage tanks, digging sump to Nissen huts at Chateau, Bus complete in shape for concrete repairs to floor, Baths. Little work on localities owing to bad weather. Other work as on 1st.	/c
	3.8.18		As on 2nd. No work on MUSTARD or SHRINE WEST Trails, no work being done on working parties being available. Pushing gas-proofing Coy HQ in CUTTING POINT completed. 38 cabs made at Bus R.E. Dump. Concreting the walls of M.G. Pill-Box now up to 3'.	/c
	4.8.18		Shelters at Battn HQ (J.34.b.2.6) completed. Road at J.23 central completely metalled, only requiring drain out metalled path. Lane to D.H.Q. 12 Nohei Bande filled at gaps as now in P.6. Remainder as yesterday.	/c
	5.8.18		As on 4th. Commenced erection of plunge bath at BERTRANCOURT BATHS - Site levelled, framing & sorting of boiler for installation at COURCELLES Baths, laying papers &c. Gas made & erected.	/c
	6.8.18		As on 5th. Work on road at J.23 central suspended. One more metal available for path.	/c
	7.8.18		Completed Coy HQ at J.23.b.9.2. Continuing work on localities & erecting of plating for garrison of same. Continuing to roof M.G. Pill Box, commenced shelter plates for plunging the BERTRANCOURT Baths in frame. Repairman water into it from storage tank. Various jobs in Bus proceeding.	/c
	8.8.18		As on 6th. Plunge bath at BERTRANCOURT nearing completion. Brickwork laid. Main 40% completed.	/c

WAR DIARY
Sheet 2
INTELLIGENCE SUMMARY

(Erase heading not required.)

Army Form C. 2118.

Instructions regarding War Diaries and Intelligence Summaries are contained in F.S. Regs. Part II. and the Staff Manual respectively. Title pages will be prepared in manuscript.

Place	Date	Hour	Summary of Events and Information	Remarks and references to Appendices
	10.8.18		Plunge bath found to leak badly & decision to put in 3 coats of tar outside & 1 coat inside pending repair made. Work on locations continued, excavation on top of site being available for last. 2 sappers continued carrying to roof of Pill Box, rainforcement of same. Preparing & filling of excavation for storage tank at COURCELLES Baths.	J/2.
	11.8.18		As on 10th. Commenced relaying tram tracks from P.S. A. 3.6. 3 curves & 50' straight work on shelters in localities held up for lack of timber.	J/2.
	12.8.18		Continued work on tram tracks, 2 curves & 30' straight relaid, work now in wrecking excavation for storage tank at Baths. COURCELLES completely rivelted sunk in position - awaiting test for engine completed, shooting parties being able unavailable, no progress made on construction of localities on approach to A.D.S.	J/2.
	13.8.18		Local engine at COURCELLES Baths. Work continued on Pill Box at J35, c.7.2. M.G. Pill Box, Shelter in MUSTARD SHRINE NEST CUTTING ORCHARD POSTS. Improvement of road to A.D.S. recommenced, test train ran over cut & 5 camps dug. Parties daily for improvement of those kinds, painting & erecting notice boards.	J/2.
	14.8.18		Camouflage screens camouflage from "MOR" Pill Box erected at J. 23. c. 95. 80, preparing for concrete roof & bringing stone on to site. Water works as on 13th.	J/2.
	15.8.18		As on 14th. Commenced fixing platform to Foden disinfector. Plunge bath at BERTRANCOURT completed, filled & now working satisfactory. Excavation for de-lousing Chamber at this Baths completed.	J/2.
	16.8.18		Concreting to roof of "MOR" Pill Box 83% completed. Remaining jobs proceeded with.	J/2.
	17.8.18		Line of proposed tramway S. of SERRE marked out. Party engaged firing in drain across track at J.20.c. 6.7. Continued concreting to roof of "MOR" Pill Box, concreting to proposed flying to M.G. Pill Box No2 at J. 35.6.76 completed, 4.2. LONGFIELD" aeroplane flares placed within flying to Pumping Chamber at COURCELLES Baths, clearing site for land trough & excavating for water bottle filler. Continued erection of de-lousing chamber at BERTRANCOURT	J/2.
	18.8.18		Concreting to roof of "MOR" Pill Box completed. Carrying out repairs to roof & walls of billet COURCELLES (J 29 d.) fixing windows with a Baths at BERTRANCOURT on shelters for parties who formerly, continued. Major Enthwaite returned from leave.	J/2.
	19.8.18		As on 18th.	J/2.

Army Form C. 2118.

Sheet 3   **WAR DIARY**

INTELLIGENCE SUMMARY.
(Erase heading not required.)

Instructions regarding War Diaries and Intelligence Summaries are contained in F. S. Regs., Part II. and the Staff Manual respectively. Title pages will be prepared in manuscript.

Place	Date	Hour	Summary of Events and Information	Remarks and references to Appendices
	20.8.18.		At on 19th. Camouflage completed to move Ree Boc. Repairs to roof of billet at COURCELLES & facing of roof of A.D.S. Party of 8 Sappers & 76 Infantry working made walls 40% complete. Casing out repairs to roof of A.D.S. Party of 8 Sappers & 76 Infantry working from 9am to 3am just repairing D.W. track in K.29.d. centre. Capt. C & Lt. Jones reported 429th Field Coy. R.E.	f.1
	21.8.18.		Practically no work done owing to operations forward tracks patrolled and repaired. Notice boards painted fixed. Excavation for trench for 4" water pipe from Bucquoi, MAILLY MAILLET. cont.	f.1
	22.8.18.		Arranged to work at night on 4" pipe main from MAILLY Bucquoi exchange. Sites (with G.O.S) storage tank (30 x 30) for gravity flow. Also sited stores watering point at Bucquoi for which W.P. to Bucquoi Junk Siding at R.M. at COURCELLES mortared and Lieut. T.E. TAYLOR proceeded to Bucquoi spot. Train been passed by R.D.M.S. scheme of the front. No stock of shingle accordingly so unfit for further use. Company moved from BUS WOODS camp to COURCELLES. AU-BOIS (Men transport which remains on BUS-SOUENCOURT Road.) 1 Section on making trench for 4" pipe from Bucquoi. 1 Section on erection of shelter for petrol engine at COURCELLES Baths.	f.1
	23.8.18.			f.1
	24.8.18.		Erection of 3 troughs at new Water Point at Bucquoi (K.32.d.9.6) & erection of 2 tents for D.H.Q. at Crock Gully (K.32.a.3.1) completed, also repair of cogs to driving wheel of pump at SUCRERIE. Lieut. L.J. MARR left Coy to proceed on leave to U.K.	f.1
	25.8.18.		Company (less transport) moved by march route from COURCELLES-AU-BOIS, through COURINCAMPS, along FUSILIER TRACK to PUISIEUX-AU-MONT (L.21.6.6.7) arriving at destination about 11.30 am. Work in afternoon repairing SERRE-PUISIEUX-MIRAUMONT Road & reaching 14 Coy A.T. Coy R.E. on Water Point, MIRAUMONT.	f.1
	26.8.18.		Transport moved from J.31.b.2.8. to Bucquoi. MAILLY MAILLET but owing to hostile arrangements proceeded again after about hour to dismounted Sections Camp at L.21.c.6.7. arriving there about 6 a.m. 3 Sections engaged on repairs to PUISIEUX-MIRAUMONT and MIRAUMONT-ACHIET-LE-PETIT Roads. Tunnelling Coy. (179th & 262nd) & 17th N.F. (P) assisted on road repairs.	f.2
	27.8.18.		2 Sections made of personnel of Tunnelling Coys Pioneers &c above continue work on road repairs on PUISIEUX-MIRAUMONT Road, demolishing bricks whilst along road with sappers running Coy road. Also K. Coy Army R.E. found at L.21.c. and at L.27b. which was made quite passable throughout. Party engaged clearing stores on R.E. Bung at MIRAUMONT (6.35.b.2.4) on completed materials for this from L.30.a. central. 1 Section on erecting new camp for D.H.Q. at L.10.a.8.9. Collecting	f.2

Army Form C. 2118.

Sheet 4.   **WAR DIARY**
INTELLIGENCE SUMMARY
(*Erase heading not required.*)

Instructions regarding War Diaries and Intelligence
Summaries are contained in F. S. Regs., Part II.
and the Staff Manual respectively. Title pages
will be prepared in manuscript.

Place	Date	Hour	Summary of Events and Information	Remarks and references to Appendices
	28.8.18		2 Sections on ugg repairs as yesterday. 10 Sappers engaged dismantling Chaine Hétice pump & Engine Thragt Pélice pump from COURCELLES, & the & transporting same to MIRAUMONT STATION DUMP. 1 Section continuing work on new B.H.Q. & Section on camp improvements, erecting Nissens hut &c. Lightboards painted & retained for erection in PUSIEUX.	/c
	29.8.18		1 Section & PYS to work under nude plus O 125 Bde in defence, but owing to advance continuing nothing was done in this respect. Arrangements in hand for transport to & erection on up 2 Sta. Chaine Hélice Pumps & Engine transport to WARLENCOURT ready for erection in U.K. 1 Lieut. G.W.LORD left to proceed on leave to U.K.	/c
	30.8.18		The whole Coy. moved by march route at 8 a.m. Coy. H.Q. & Sappers moving to M.3.c.7.7 (between IRLES and WARLENCOURT- EAUCOURT) and Transport. Lines to MIRAUMONT. No 3 Section went on detachment to 125th Inf. Bde. in 29 Sect. for purpose of digging defensive localities nr. LOUPART WOOD. Nomes Rd. Coy. 1 Section went to WARLENCOURT & erected pump engine taken there last night at Well No. 3. for Chaine Héline Pump. Then Two-fold troops. 1 Section at Well No. 2 & levelled funnel for Chaine 54 pumping nunow. power pump from Well No. 1 & erected complete at Well No. 2. Remaining Section engaged on erection of new B.H.Q. in G.30.c. Owing to enemy shelling at MIRAUMONT water points, arranged to erect 2,200 gallon tank in M.2.d. at well next being dug there. also arranged to dig new well in the PYS- IRLES valley.	/c
	31.8.18		Work proceeded at No. 3 well, WARLENCOURT, where there is 17ft 5 inches of water and the pump engine as capable of delivering 500 gallons per hour. Work commenced on Spray bath and 2 water cart filling points and 1 water cattle filling point. 2 Sections R.E. assisted by 2 Platoons of this work. 2 Sappers still employed at pumping Station at MAILLY MAILLET. Patrols found for MIRAUMONT W.P.S. watering points. One R.D. Rate (wounded) evacuated to Head Veterinary Section.	/c

Strength of Compy. on 1/9/18. Officers 8. 204 OR.
                              31/8/18.   6 " 200 OR.

8 OR reinforcements joined Compy. during month.
No battle casualties during month.
(sickness etc. being only cause.)

P.T.O.

WAR DIARY
INTELLIGENCE SUMMARY.

Army Form C. 2118.

Place	Date	Hour	Summary of Events and Information	Remarks and references to Appendices
			Drawings Attached:—	
			Sheet 57 D	
			Machine Gun Emplacement No 2 at J.30.b.7.6.	
			do No. 1. and J at J.30.b.7.6.	
			Observation Post.	

Major

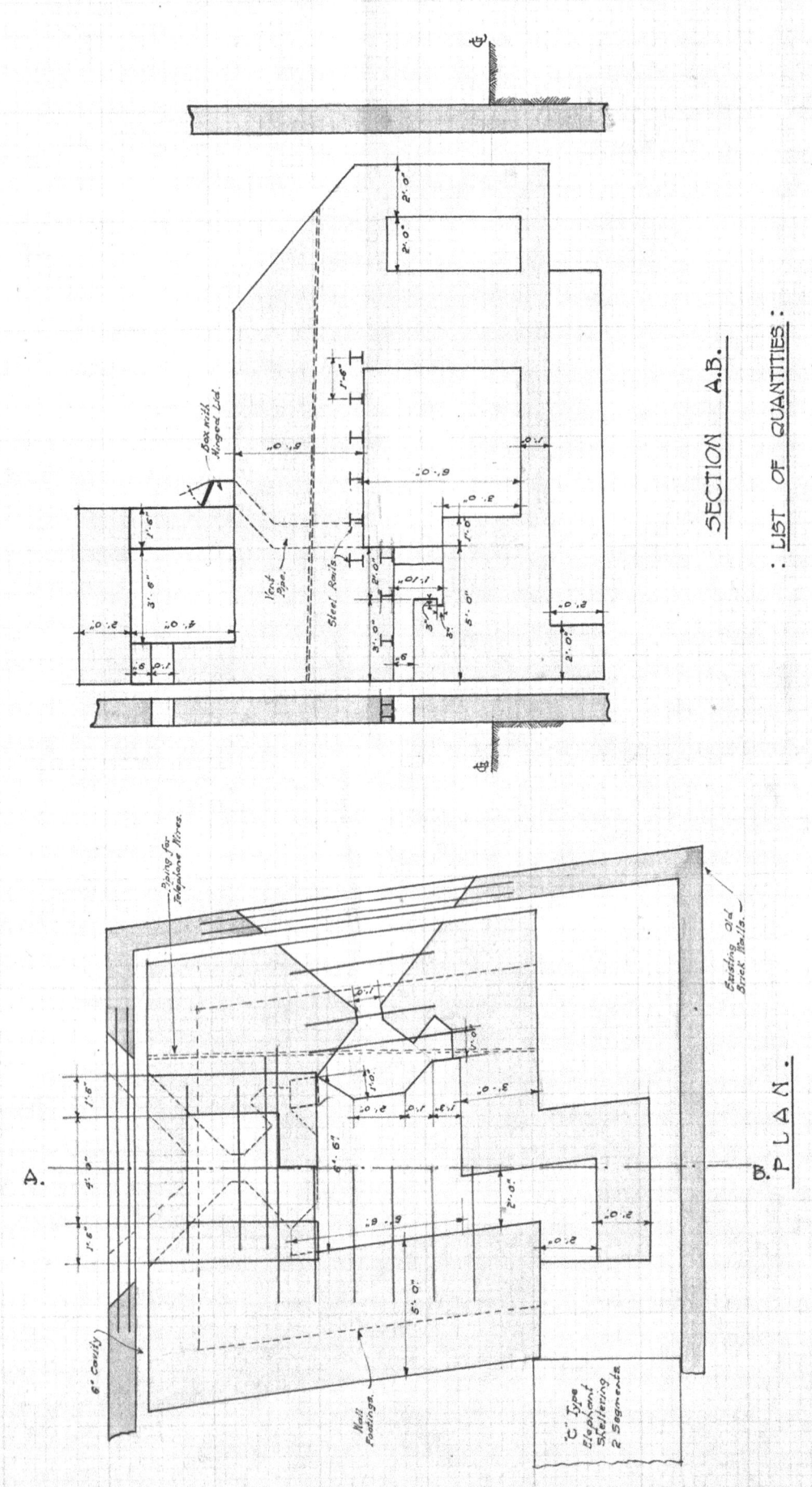

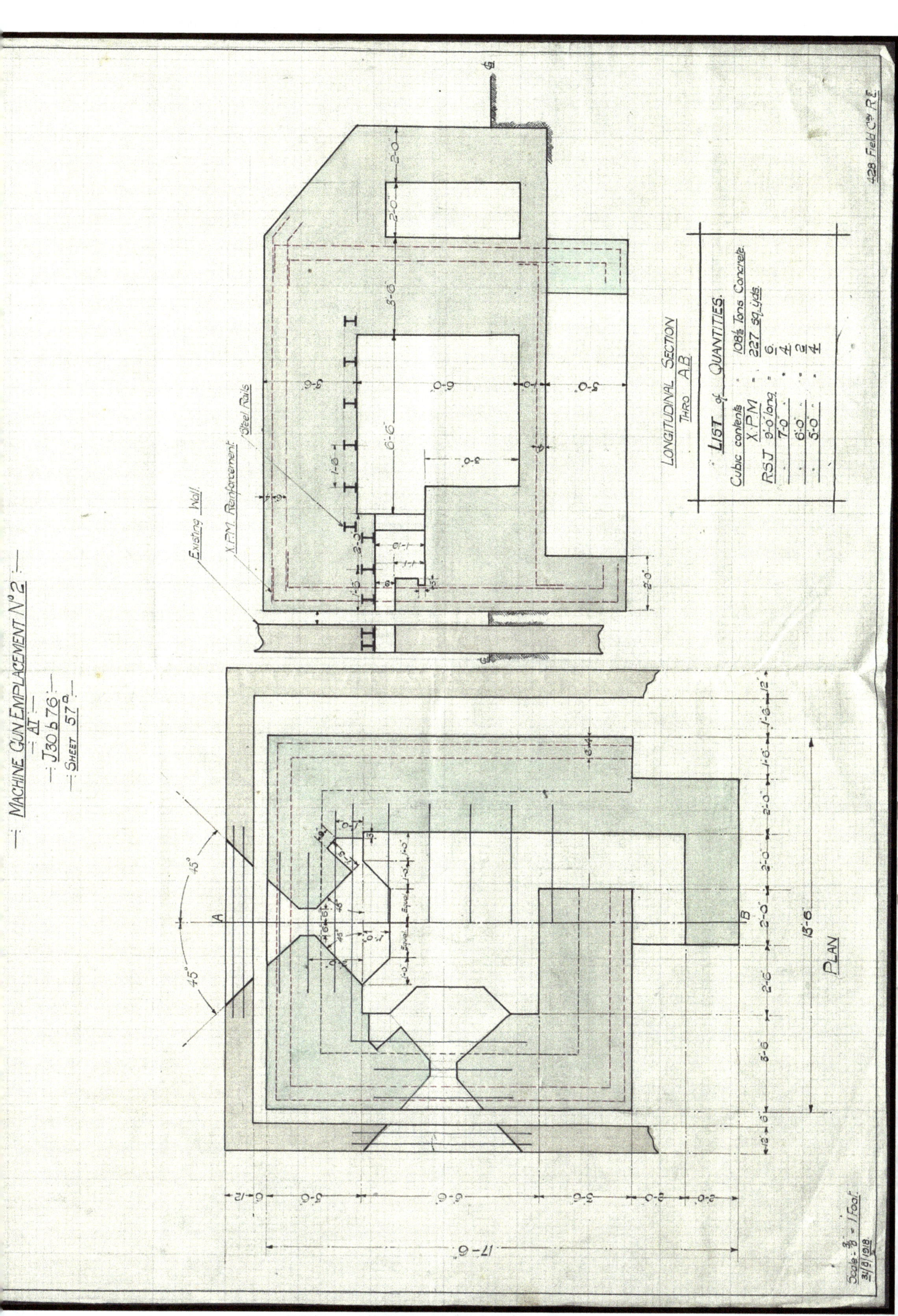

MACHINE GUN EMPLACEMENT No 1 AND OBSERVATION POST.

AT J.30.b.7.6.   SHEET 57D.

SECTION A.B.

PLAN.

SCALE. FOUR FEET TO ONE INCH.

LIST OF QUANTITIES:

Cubic Contents	3077 c.ft. = **165** Tons Concrete.	
Steel Joists.	12'.0" long.	4.
Ditto ditto.	10'.0" do.	6.
Ditto ditto.	7'.0" do.	2.
Ditto ditto.	6'.0" do.	4.

428 Field Co. R.E.

31.8.18.

Labels on drawing: Boxwith Hinged Lid, Vent Pipe, Steel Rails, Spring for Telephone Wires, Existing Old Brick No.1/a, 6" Cavity, Wall Footings, "C" Type Elephant Sheltering 2 Segments.

Army Form C. 2118.

WAR DIARY
INTELLIGENCE SUMMARY.
(Erase heading not required.)

Sheet 1.

Original Vol 20

428TH (EAST LANCS) FIELD COY. R.E.

Place	Date	Hour	Summary of Events and Information	Remarks and references to Appendices
	1.9.18		Company HdQrs & 4 dismounted sections camped at M.3.c.75.70 (between PYS and WARLENCOURT-EAUCOURT. Transport lines at MIRAUMONT. Coy. engaged on erection of huts sectionmen 42 at new D.H.Q. in G.30.c. (GREVILLERS) also at Water points at WARLENCOURT-EAUCOURT (wells No 2 & 3) erecting hoses from the storage tanks, forming truck standings, fixing pumps, repairing engines etc. also clearing approaches. Also at 4000 gallon tank to PYS well (No 1) to be got up tonight for Lorries. also started to well. 8 PYS Well No 2 single water frame to supplies windlass fixed for 2 water cart fillers with standards. These erected at No 2 Well MARLENCOURT Tank erected almost complete during day. 1 Pichon N.F.(P) 4 wellies site of Bath at No 2 well.	/c
	2.9.18		No.2 & 3 Sections employed WARLENCOURT BATHS which were complete during the day, & moving iron adrift. Flume to Water Cart & water Bottle filler completed. PYS Well (M.2.d.50.85) - a second 600 gall trough erected, making 600F.H. double through filling. PYS Well (M.3.a.9.9.) - framing carried, well abandoned in consequence of all tanks being taken out.	/c
	3.9.18		Mounted section Transport moves from MIRAUMONT Standing bay at M.3.c.75.70. PYS Well No 4 at M.2.d.50.85. Completed flagged surface. PYS Pond watering point PYS Well No 3, and MIRAUMONT No 3, water points delivery completed. Lorries dismantled & 2350 gall. & 1 - 30 x 30 tank from M.C.64.0. ready for erection at BAPAUME ...	/c
	4.9.18		Company moved Transport to THILLOY. dismantled sections to eastern edge of VILLERS-AU-FLOS work (Q.8.c.4.5.). 1 Section engaged in erection of storage tanks at BAPAUME Waterpoint. 2 Section engaged in erection of PETIT-L&G Lyne Pump at GRENCOURT Well. (N.5.d.5.) Mainly continuing completed erection of well & 230 gall tank. Growth was obtained at 2 moving to small party engaged at Putting up pipes & fixing ... at R.BAPAUME - BREGNUS Rd in N.5.c. Working alongside of action water supplies arriving to small parties turning to be dropped during around. ie in Rolls Rois and Bus. Pumping house at MARILET Erecene. R.E. Group to ACHIET-LE-PETIT. Water Points at MIRAUMONT WARLENCOURT.	/E
	5.9.18		Work continues at GRENCOURT WELL. Engine base completed. Write bottle filler. (400 gall tank) erected, work house to well. Stairfase of 22 All huts completed, with 2 water only standards for Ramps approaches, starting. From troughs completed, with my assistance of appointed N.F.(P) Rinsen and platelins further in Famel to Lie. the Coy. N.Z.E.	/c
	6.9.18		The whole company moved into both Camp at M.3.c.75.70, marching in rear of 100 ? HQ R.E.	/s

(A7092) Wt. W12859/M1293 75.70.0. 1/17. D. D. & L., Ltd. Forms/C.2118/44.

Army Form C. 2118.

Original

Sheet 2

WAR DIARY
or
INTELLIGENCE SUMMARY
(Erase heading not required.)

Place	Date	Hour	Summary of Events and Information	Remarks and references to Appendices
	7.9.18		Company resting with exception of 1 section which worked in erection of hut for Brit Canteen, & stage for Brit Concert Party	/=
	8.9.18		Also on 7th. Drawing room attached to Divs Hdrs Coy attended Church Parade. Erecting harness sheds etc. in Coy Transport Lines. Huts at 127th Fld HQ, & foot drying chamber at HAVRINCOURT Chateau.	/=
	9.9.18		Training Carried on, principally gun drill musketry Lewis gun instruction. Afternoon devoted to Recreational training. L Promotion party water supply mostly from MIRAUMONT returned that to shell. L Man reported from leave in U.K.	/=
	10.9.18			/=
	11.9.18		As on 11th. Lewis Gun Instructor on Musketry instruction attached from 127th Inf. Bde. A careful inspection of gas equipment was held & men passes through Gas Chamber. A design was made for Anderson Lrr Prot. Scatter Spar 35, using only 1 trenching round. Tarpaulin to cover same aimed for with CRE.	/=
	12.9.18		As on 12th.	/=
	13.9.18		Training continued. Assistance given to Batt n of 127 Inf Bde in erecting Bombard Bivouacs.	/=
	14.9.18		Church Parade in morning. 2/Lieut Lord Wemyss Company farm leave in U.K. Training continued as before. Divisional Sports completed.	/=
	15.9.18			/=
	16.9.18		As on 16th.	/=
	17.9.18		As on 17th. 2 Officers no Lester Engrs visited work in hand by 152 & 7th Coy R.E. between HAVRINCOURT WOOD & TRESCAULT	/=
	18.9.18			/=
	19.9.18		Training continued. Transport Officer inspected Type Lines of 153 with Coy at RUYAULCOURT who has taken over from 152 R.E. Coy. Reconnaissance party (1 Offcr & 6 I.R. to take over Billets at 153 Fd Coy in HAVRINCOURT WOOD (P.12.b.5.6) arriving Rue at 1.30 pm.	/=
	20.9.18		Company moved by march route to 1/2 BUSQUIERE (12.8.b.70) Dept Officer to BERTINCOURT to view Horse Lines site	/=
	21.9.18		March was continued (Dismounted Sections only) to camp of 153rd Coy at P.12.b.50 Transport & Mounted Section to P.2.b.1.8. Parties at my post on work clearing repairing TRESCAULT WELL (Q.10.a.4.6) working in 6 hour shifts round the clock.	/=
	22.9.18		Minor repairs made at 126th Inf Bde H.Q. Geo graphical depots at various points (1 Section) Gas proof Curbs fitted to water trunks in Forward area (1 Section) Remainder of Btl in a depth of Y.16th now resting	/=

(A7091. Wt W12859/M1293. 75.10.0. 4/17. D. D. & L., Ltd. Forms/C.2118/14.)

Army Form C. 2118.

Sheet 3

Original

WAR DIARY
INTELLIGENCE SUMMARY
(Erase heading not required.)

Instructions regarding War Diaries and Intelligence Summaries are contained in F.S. Regs, Part II. and the Staff Manual respectively. Title pages will be prepared in manuscript.

Place	Date	Hour	Summary of Events and Information	Remarks and references to Appendices
	23.9.18		Fitted cover to 30% tank at D.7. a. 7.1. 2 parties organised for reconnaissance & gas proofing dugouts near the whole Brigade Front. 2 feet of water now obtained at TRESCAULT WELL.	
	24.9.18		Reconnaissance & proofing of dugouts continued as yesterday. 2 parties upwards of 40 dugouts faced & lichit hatch of Dudley off well as dwist ingots so as to keep air. Lieut. W.— let down to chamber. 2/Lieut NEAD left company for 10 days leave in U.K. Parties at various points & holes in Forward Area. Parties & N.C.Os. engaged on dugout reconnaissance reporting in Q.2, Q.3, Q.4, Q.10, & K.33 & 34. 25 Blankets fixed during the day. Chambers at TRESCAULT WELL extended to 10 × 7 × 7.	
	25.9.18		Dugout at Welsh Station at 126th Bde. H.Q. Strengthened. Gas proofing continued. Remainder as on previous days.	
	26.9.18		Operations began at 5.20 a.m. 2 parties & Engineers reported at Bn. reliefs Bde. H.Q. in order to mark out tracks as the situation allowed. 1 Sergt. was eventually marked at B. Left Bde. front. 8 Sappers were attached to B.H.Ps. for Booby Trap work. 2 parties for dugout reconnaissance a large number of dugouts in front of the HINDENBURG front-support lines. Engr. pump located. Well sported at TRESCAULT, & assistance given to 149 A.T. Coy in examination. 2 Parties also on dugout reconnaissance in captured areas. Q.9.6, Q.11, & Q.12. men L.31, L.32, & L.36 respectively. 20 gas blankets were fixed. Demountable torch lamp taken to P.O.B.72 & transferred to TRESCAULT for addition at Hell Keel. 5 Enemy Coy. mined (of the 10 sapper type) discovered at x Ravine in TRESCAULT & removed (Q.10, a, 4, 9). Arrangements made & more Coy. to be neighbourhood of K.36 Central, or being warned for attachment to 126 Bde. for exploitation purposes. These and others were carried later, on warning of relief by N.Z. Division.	
	27.9.18		Engineer reconnaissance parties again employed in same areas. As Mobile Bgde sucked at park in captured areas well reconnaissance at RIBÉCOURT — 3 Wells found & decided 5 explain the one at L.25.c.75. Tramways & shifts & sprs. still engaged in dispersing well at TRESCAULT. Reconnaissance report complete in BEAUCAMP (Q.26.c+d). Command work at Sucrerie framing complete before nightfall. 12 Sappers set (cook's) bivouacs from YVEU Dump. to site.	
	28.9.18		Work continued on dugout & surveys of tramways. Well but owing to Enemy flying to RSPD with line down little work was done. Work proceeded all morning little additional Engr. fittings obtained & installation restored to completion. 12 hour lasar from twenty nine pts. L.25.d.25.33. (RIBECOURT) as attempted this is out of Divisional Area. The manufactory plate of officers at Trescault necessitates moves of watering points being formed elsewhere. Strength 30 O.R. 1 Officer 20% O.R. Band Evacuation:— 1 O.T. wounded (slight) at duty 3 O.R. " " evacuated to Hospital.	

ORIGINAL
Army Form C. 2118.

WAR DIARY

INTELLIGENCE SUMMARY
(Erase heading not required.)

SHEET 1.

Instructions regarding War Diaries and Intelligence Summaries are contained in F.S. Regs., Part II. and the Staff Manual respectively. Title pages will be prepared in manuscript.

428th FIELD COMPANY. R.E.

Place	Date	Hour	Summary of Events and Information	Remarks and references to Appendices
Coy. H.Q. & Dismounted Camp Pts. b. 5.0 (HAVRINCOURT WOOD) Transport Lines BERTINCOURT.	1-10-18		Party continued on Baths at TRESCAULT (Q.10.a.4.6.) Pipe line laid, duckboards fixed & forms to stoves fitted – it is now completed. 5 contact mines were found and removed by this party from road junction at Q.4.d.2.0. Shaft of dugout runner road at K.36 & 77 was strengthened with timber, and roadway made good. Gang also erected and L.&S pumps installed at K.30.a.1.0 & L.25.d.25.35. The party employed also removed 6 Tank Traps from Q.3.a.9.9. 1 Section assisting 149th A.T. Coy. R.E. awaiting Pipe Line & laying pipes from Q.14.d.8.1. to Q.26.c.1.4. Reconnaissance made of TRESCAULT Run Road from MASNIERES to CREVECOEUR. 40 charges extracted from Road Bridges at G.28.b.2.0 & G.34.a.2.9.	
	2.10.18		Party continued repairing A.T. Coy. R.E. of Pipe Line. Wells at K.30.a.1.0 and L.25.d.25.35. cleaned & repaired & a strong flow of water obtained at the latter. Reconnaissance made of wells in VILLERS PLOUICH and LA VACQUERIE. 1 Section clearing drain filling pot-holes on TRESCAULT – RIBECOURT ROAD. Officer i/c for 126th Infantry Bde. at Q.8.d.2.6. Commenced also a memorial for South Wing - Rt. HAVRINCOURT. Transport Lines moved to Q.13.d.O.G. (S. of HAVRINCOURT WOOD).	
	3-10-18		Officers Mess & themselves completed. Party employed on dismantling of water points at Q.15.a.3.0. Q.7.c.57. & Q.8.a.05. & pump, hose, hanging to stored in R.E. Dump. Other work as yesterday.	
	4.10.18		Dismounted portion of Coy. moved to TRESCAULT (Q4.c.4.G.) Party employed digging latrines, building cookhouse & generally improving Gen. Camp. 67 O.R. repairs to TRESCAULT – RIBECOURT ROAD, with 3 F.E. Wagons & 2 Scotch lorries removing supply. Continued work on wells at RIBECOURT (L.25.d.20,23 and L.25.d. 20.25). Steam Roller pump & engine dismantled & handed over to 149 A.T. Coy. R.E. at BERTINCOURT	
	5.10.18		Field pump & engine transported from BERTINCOURT to wells at RIBECOURT, erected & moved to new position. Work continued at TRESCAULT. RIBECOURT ROAD. 8 O.R. built Guardhouse at Coy. Transport Lines & commenced erection of harness Shed. Remainder of Coy. clearing Camp &c. Capt. A.N. WALKER rejoined Company at night.	
	6.10.18		As on 5th. Engine pump at RIBECOURT Well working in evening. Erection of Engine house commenced. Major V. ENTWISTLE left Coy. to proceed to H.Q. R.E. to take over work as G.C.R.E. Personnel not detailed for jobs were given instruction in use of Lewis Gun in afternoon.	

WAR DIARY

INTELLIGENCE SUMMARY.
(Erase heading not required.)

Army Form C. 2118.

SHEET 2

Instructions regarding War Diaries and Intelligence Summaries are contained in F. S. Regs., Part II. and the Staff Manual respectively. Title pages will be prepared in manuscript.

Place	Date	Hour	Summary of Events and Information	Remarks and references to Appendices
	7.10.18		Erection of Engine Houses at RIBECOURT well continued. 2 Sections employed forming a standard trestle at TRESCAULT RD. dump - all timber cut to lock-bolted for bolts. Remainder of Coy. standing by & were given further practice with Lewis Gun.	
	8.10.18		1 Section (N.B.C.) attached to 126 Light Rly. for work reconnaissance in forward area. Always satisfactory. Lashings continued at G.I. to L. of pump in a minute line. Water and am. still effect at x.25.d.20.25 & pumping hard. Shafting fixed way down well at x.25.d.20.25 to reduce lift of pump to 6 mins. Pump & came now be fixed in 6 minutes at this well.	
	9.10.18		Company with transport left TRESCAULT & proceeded by march route via VILLERS PLOUICH & LA VACQUERIE to M.B.C. Shelters for midday meal, proceeding later via M.12.a.1.9, via LESDAIN. Bivouac at RIBECOURT picked up standard beams to Water Supply Dump at I.33.c.1.9.	VILLERS PLOUICH & LA VACQUERIE Water Supply.
	10.10.18		1 Section developing Water Supply at ESNES, Troughs made & standards erected & pumps fixed. 1 Section engaged dismantling for Mine Booty Dumps in ESNES. Remainder (less detached section) standing by & doing odd jobs on camp improvement.	
	11.10.18		Parties employed approaching water points, dismantling pontoon bridges from ESCAUT RIVER & canal, loading same & transporting to JEUNE BOIS, near CAUDRY. Completing water points at ESNES.	ESCAUT RIVER & CAUDRY.
	12.10.18		Company with Transport moved by march route to JEUNE BOIS (I.11.Cent.) on CAMBRAI-LE-CATEAU RD. Work commenced at noon in development of Water Point at BEAUVOIS. Water supply at BEAUVOIS. Better engine required. Dismantling & erection of 2000 gall. tank commenced. Water Point at AUXICOURT FARM. - Dismantling pipe line & collecting engine stores. Party on camp improvements, fixing Horse lines & digging latrines &c.	
	13.10.18		Work continued on Water Point Development, BEAUVOIS Brasserie - 2000 gall. tank & 600; gall. tank erected & installation of Petter engine simplified. General Bailey's engine commenced. AUXICOURT FARM - Tank brought through channel. Sides & bottom but not satisfactory. Water pumped out being insufficient for requirements, a Petter Engine therefore installed. JEUNE BOIS - 600 gall. tank erected.	
	14.10.18		Water supply work continued, together with renovation of baths at Brasserie, BEAUVOIS. Installation of Baths at AUXICOURT FARM. Petter Engine at Brasserie, BEAUVOIS, found unsatisfactory two dismantled. Steam plant already in place taken into use.	
	15.10.18		As yesterday, with addition of installation of Water Point at HERPIGNY FARM.	
	16.10.18		Development of Water Points continued. Detailed reconnaissance for Water Supply at NESLY commenced. Pumping tests made at water points to elimination of those not required. Station attached to 126 FC Bde. employed on new Water Point at PRAYELLE, preparing bricks & plaster brought for the purpose.	
	17.10.18		As yesterday & in addition loading NZE bridging equipment & transporting same to PRAYELLE R.E. DUMP.	

ORIGINAL

Army Form C. 2118.

SHEET 3.

WAR DIARY
of
INTELLIGENCE SUMMARY.
(Erase heading not required.)

Instructions regarding War Diaries and Intelligence Summaries are contained in F. S. Regs., Part II. and the Staff Manual respectively. Title pages will be prepared in manuscript.

Place	Date	Hour	Summary of Events and Information	Remarks and references to Appendices
	18.10.18		Development of various water points pushed on with all speed in readiness for forthcoming operations. 3 Sections employed on water supply at VIESLY and BRIASTRE	
	19.10.18			
	20.10.18		As yesterday. Troughs, tanks, water cart fillers, pumps &c fixed at various points. Little work on water supply development at BRIASTRE owing to heavy enemy shelling. One officer reccn. on Reconnaissance work E. of River SELLE.	
	21.10.18		Work as on 20th. Erection of Baths commenced at BRIASTRE, but notice received to cease, as village being handed over to 37th Division. Repairs effected to trough pumps at JAUNE BOIS, BEAUVOIS BRIASTRE & AULICOURT FARM.	
	22.10.18		Baths already erected at BRIASTRE dismantled. Stores returned to R.E. Dump, PRAYELLE. Small alterations made to Water points at AULICOURT FARM and PRAYELLE. Work at VIESLY finished & handed over to 142 A.T. Coy R.E. Reconnaissance made of OLD CARDON MILL (E.2.C. and d.) (not E. of GOUSSNES.)	
	23.10.18		Small party employed patrolling water points, effecting alterations & repairs where necessary. Remainder of Company cleaning up neatly.	
	24.10.18		As on 23rd. Repairs to pumps carried out. 8 men employed running engines at water points	
	25.10.18		As on 24th.	
	26.10.18		Party collecting materials for Divisional Boxing Ring. Remainder training.	
	27.10.18		As on 26th. Training.	
	28.10.18		1 Section employed making floor for dining room at Divl. Reception Camp, & covering good-all tank at AULICOURT FARM. 1 Section ordering timber, running stores for Boxing Ring & Sounding Board. Making sign-boards & Reminder training.	
	29.10.18		As on 28th.	
	30.10.18		Pants completed erection of Boxing Ring. Round Board at Divl. Theatre, staking down 2 partitions. 15 O.R. completed work on floor at Reception Camp at AULICOURT FARM, made 2 name signs, & covered remainder of frame for Ring with wire netting. Preparations for Bihut Contest Ground.	
	31.10.18		Preparations for Divl. R.E. Horse Show and Sports. Moved Section Medical Inspection Officer to Bnde Comdr. E. of 126 Infy Bde. Wing. an of Runs Contest Ground.	

Casualties:— Joined Coy, during month { 1 Off. } Strength on 1/10/18 Y.off. 204 o.R.
                                           { 12 o.R. }   31/10/18 Y.off. 195 o.R.
              Left Comptr during the month { 21 o.R. }

No Battle Casualties during the month.

(A7093) Wt. W12839/M1295. 75,000. 1/17. D. D. & L., Ltd. Forms/C.2118/24.

428th Coy R.E.
SHEET 1
Army Form C. 2118.

WAR DIARY

INTELLIGENCE SUMMARY

Ref. Map. Belgium & Part of France
Sheets 57, 57A, 51 1/20,000

Place	Date	Hour	Summary of Events and Information	Remarks and references to Appendices
JEUNE BOIS	1-11-18		Company and Transport lines still at JEUNE BOIS on CAMBRAI — LE CATEAU Road. 42nd Divisional R.E. sports held in a field at PREMELLE. Whole Company attended.	A.N.W.
	2-11-18		Improvements effected at Divisional Theatre, BERUVOIS, taking down existing walls and increasing accommodation. Setting out and signboarding of ground for Divisional Band Contest, and laying wooden platform on Divisional football ground.	A.N.W.
	3-11-18		Company preparing for move and for forthcoming advance. Vehicles loaded and explosives tested.	A.N.W.
	4-11-18		Company complete with transport moved to SOLESMES by march route via VIESLY and BRIASTRE leaving 09.00 and arriving at 12.30, and rested remainder of day.	A.N.W.
SOLESMES	5-11-18		Company including transport moved at 09.30 to LE QUESNOY in pouring rain, arriving about 16.00. Two officers sent forward to make forward reconnaissances for water supply in region of LE QUESNOY, LE CARNOY and HERBIGNIES. One officer with advance party sent on ahead to decide whether situation would allow the Company to be billeted in LE QUESNOY.	A.N.W.
LE QUESNOY	6-11-18		Company with transport moved at 09.00 to LE CARNOY arriving about 13.30. Three officers sent out on road reconnaissances in FORET DE MORMAL with object of ascertaining possible route to take forward bridging equipment if situation allowed the bridging of the River SAMBRE. At 16.00 orders received for Continuous work on divisional bridge over Brown Culvert at N.29.a.8.4. Sections detailed in 6 hour shifts commencing 16.00, and transport turned out to take up 1 Weldon trestle and 2 bays superstructure from MAISON ROUGE to site of work.	A.N.W.
LE CARNOY	7-11-18		Divisional bridge ready for traffic at 06.00 and maintained during the day, being subject to a constant stream of traffic and several times broken. At 12.30 Company ordered to move at 14.00 with transport to vicinity of PETIT BAYAY. Dismounted portion (less 1 section) arrived about 17.00	A.N.W.

SHEET 2

Army Form C. 2118.

Ref Maps: Belgium & Northern France.
Sheets 57, 57A & 57. 1:40,000.

WAR DIARY
INTELLIGENCE SUMMARY.
(Erase heading not required.)

Instructions regarding War Diaries and Intelligence Summaries are contained in F. S. Regs., Part II. and the Staff Manual respectively. Title pages will be prepared in manuscript.

Place	Date	Hour	Summary of Events and Information	Remarks and references to Appendices
LA CORNE	8-11-18		T billeted at LA CORNE (V.3.a.1.9). Transport arrived later & remaining section rejoined during the night.	
			Company rested in morning and received orders at 12.30 to send out 2 Sections to HAUTMONT to take out any mines and booby traps. Sections given other orders on the march by C.R.E. & one halted at VIEUX MESNIL and looked for billets for whole Company, and the other proceeded to NEUF MESNIL and looked for billets for dismounted portion of Company. At 15.30 orders for Company with transport to move to HAUTMONT. Transport moved only as far as Eastern edge of FORET de MORMAL (O.28.d.1.6).	A.N.W.
Various.	9.11.18.		Dismounted portion of Company concentrated at HAUTMONT and at 10.00 commenced bridging the River SAMBRE. Twelve 7 stud joists found in neighbourhood and a bridge 18'-6" span erected over locks. A bridge consisting of 2 Wooden Trestles and 2 Pontoons was erected over river and whole completed and ready for traffic by 20.00. French Civilian Labour employed for transporting stones out for renewing a large coal dump and obstacle to one of the approaches. Transport moved up to whole Company billeted at night in HAUTMONT.	A.N.W.
HAUTMONT.	10.11.18.		Footbridge across R. Sambre (Prob.) over debris of demolished bridge commenced, and also stones collected for a bridge strong enough to carry Tanks across Lock.	A.N.W.
	11.11.18.		Footbridge completed and girders laid referred for Tank bridge. Old German Baths examined and water supply obtained from well in adjacent Brasserie. Brasserie boiler stoked up & water obtained for baths. Party turned out at night to repair damaged pontoon bridge at Hautmont.	A.N.W.

WAR DIARY

Sheet 3

Army Form C. 2118.

INTELLIGENCE SUMMARY

(Erase heading not required)

Instructions regarding War Diaries and Intelligence Summaries are contained in F.S. Regs., Part II and the Staff Manual respectively. Title pages will be prepared in manuscript.

Place	Date	Hour	Summary of Events and Information	Remarks and references to Appendices
HAUTMONT	12-11-18		Erection of Tank Bridge at Birks in HAUTMONT continued, 90% decking completed. 4 Support engaged running of plant at Birks in HAUTMONT Brasserie. 1 Section on maintenance of pontoon Bridge at BOUSSIERES. 1 Section employed reconnoissance of empty transport lines to move transport lines to new site occupied by remainder of company. 6 OR accompanied transport to pick up dump of Stores left at H.E. convoy.	E.
	13-11-18		Remainder resting after nights work on Bridge repairs. Work on Tank Bridge on Brks at HAUTMONT proceeded. Sections taken for new Long Bridge to replace Pontoon Bridge which was again broken down at 1600. 1 Section salving Pontoon equipment from River SAMBRE. Parties on erection of cookhouses and mess at Billets. Running plant at Birks.	E.
	14-11-18		Tank Bridge completed, with wheel guides and handrails. 2 Sections employed Dismantling Pontoon Bridge and collecting Stores for Long Bridge. 1 Section at 142 A.T. coy R.E. awaiting Portable engine at Factory Feately formed to the in running order. 1 Section at transport Line cleaning vehicles. cycling boots huts, ovens, latrines &c. Permanent parties employed at Birks on Bridge maintenance.	E.
	15-11-18		As yesterday. Party facing Stores at D.H.Q. 2 Bridges at MAUBEUGE visited which may be taken over in near future.	E.
	16-11-18		Erection of Long Bridge at communications project abandoned for the moment. Continued work at Birks, Brasserie, D.H.Q., transport, bridge maintenance &c.	E.
	17-11-18		As on 16th. Work on Company completed.	E.
	18-11-18		Small parties on improvements at Brit. theatre- glass sounding roof covered in windows, doors repaired, orchestra well seats, Lectures made, Lighting shed for harvey lighting power unit. Section employed on improving by vehicle.	E.
	19-11-18		As on 18th.	E.
	20-11-18		As on 19th.	E.
	21-11-18		Section at transport lines repairing driven Wells &c. 2 Sections dismantling Pontoon bridge at BOUSSIERE, packing up vehicles, transport to Bridging Dump. 3 OR overhauled rheostat heating apparatus at Brit theatre.	E.

Army Form C. 2118.

Sheet 4.

WAR DIARY

INTELLIGENCE SUMMARY.

(Erase heading not required.)

Instructions regarding War Diaries and Intelligence Summaries are contained in F.S. Regs., Part II. and the Staff Manual respectively. Title pages will be prepared in manuscript.

Place	Date	Hour	Summary of Events and Information	Remarks and references to Appendices
HAUTMONT	22-11-18		Improvements to Transport Lines & Coy. Billets continued. Heating apparatus at D.R.S. HAUTMONT examined with view to putting plant in running order.	
	23-11-18		1 Section constructing stocks at Transport Lines, cleaning rubbish from vicinity of drivers billets &c. Remainder of Coy. exercised in route march to FERRIÈRE-LE-GRAND.	
	24-11-18		Stocks at Transport Lines completed. Remainder reaching & recreational games.	
	25-11-18		Party working on construction of boxing ring for Divl. Competition. Switchboards, footlights &c. at Divl. Theatre.	
	26-11-18		As on 25th. Section on Horse Lines constructing incinerator, washing pontoons, &c.	
	27-11-18		Do on 26th.	
	28-11-18		As on 27th. Work at Divl. Theatre & boxing ring continued. 4 O.R. making coffins.	
	29-11-18		As on 28th. Those not employed on work exercised in short route march during morning. Recreational training in afternoon.	
	30-11-18		1 Section employed on destruction of German explosives, mainly PERDITE, at factory HAUTMONT. 1 Section on improvements to Transport Lines. Remainder training.	

No battle casualties during month.

Strength of Compy. on 1/11/18 : 7 Officers 195 O.R.
— do — — do — on 30/11/18 : 7 Officers 195 O.R.
2 O.R. joined Company during month.
2 O.R. Struck off Strength "

Vol 23

WAR DIARY

OF

428th (E. Lancs) Field Coy. R.E.

from 1st to 31st December. 1918

(Volume 5)

Contemporaneous
ORIGINAL

WAR DIARY
INTELLIGENCE SUMMARY

(Erase heading not required.)

Army Form C. 2118.

Ref. Maps. VALENCIENNES } 1:100,000.
NAMUR

Instructions regarding War Diaries and Intelligence Summaries are contained in F.S. Regs., Part II. and the Staff Manual respectively. Title pages will be prepared in manuscript.

Place	Date	Hour	Summary of Events and Information	Remarks and references to Appendices
HAUTMONT.	1-12-18		Field Coy billeted in HAUTMONT; employed on training in morning and recreational training in afternoon. Party attended visit of His Majesty the King.	JMW
	2-12-18 to 5-12-18		Company still on short training together with a number of small jobs at Divisional Baths & Laundry.	JMW
	6-12-18		No 2 Section with Section transport moved as advanced party to CHARLEROI via BINCHE and FONTAINE L'EVEQUE staying one night in each under orders of Major HANMER, J.C. 427 Field Coy RE. No 1 Section with Section transport moved to VIEUX RENG to carry out work of bridging orders time and at ELESMES.	JMW
	7-12-18 to 9-12-18		Remaining Sections employed on Camp duties and cleaning vehicles and lending assistance on Transport lines.	JMW
	10-12-18.		No 3 Section moved by motor-lorry to CHARLEROI, coming under orders of Major HANMER	JMW
	11-12-18.		Remainder of Company employed on cleaning vehicles and helping on Transport lines owing to shortage of drivers.	JMW
	12-12-18.		No 1 Section moved from ELESMES to CHARLEROI coming under orders of Major HANMER. No 3 Section, under orders of Major HANMER moved from CHARLEROI to FLEURUS	JMW
	13-12-18.		Remainder of Company prepared for forthcoming move, odd jobs were done for D.H.Q. and Divisional Theatre and pontoon equipment sorted out, loaded and spare on complete with superstructure sent up to MARPENT for 427 Field Coy RE. Empty wagons returning during night. Advance party of 1 Officer and 20 ORs proceeded to LAMERIES	JMW

Army Form C. 2118.

WAR DIARY
INTELLIGENCE SUMMARY.
(Erase heading not required.)

Instructions regarding War Diaries and Intelligence Summaries are contained in F.S. Regs., Part II. and the Staff Manual respectively. Title pages will be prepared in manuscript.

Ref. Maps. VALENCIENNES } 1:100,000
NAMUR

Place	Date	Hour	Summary of Events and Information	Remarks and references to Appendices
HAUTMONT	14-12-18		Remainder of Coy, Coy Hdqrs and transport moved under orders of G.O.C. 126th Inf. Bde to LAMERIES and billeted there for the night. Advance party moved to BINCHE.	Nil
LAMERIES	15-12-18		Coy Hdqrs etc moved with 126th Inf. Bde to BINCHE and billeted there for the night. Advanced party moved to FONTAINE L'EVEQUE.	Nil
BINCHE	16-12-18		Coy Hdqrs etc moved as above to FONTAINE L'EVEQUE and billeted there. Advanced party moved to CHARLEROI.	Nil
FONTAINE L'EVEQUE	17-12-18		Coy Hdqrs etc resting.	Nil
	18-12-18		Coy Hdqrs etc moved to CHARLEROI, the dismounted portion being billeted in the Jesuit College and the transport in a factory in DAMPREMY. Command of Sections 1,2+3 taken over again by O.C. 428 Field Coy. R.E.	Nil
CHARLEROI	19-12-18		Company working as follows. 1 Section at FLEURUS on work for 127th Inf. Bde. 1 Section working for R.A. 2 Sections working for D.H.Q., Coy H.Q. and transport lines. Working in all cases being installation of latrines, cookhouses, beds, tables and similar improvements for comfort of the troops.	Nil
	20-12-18 to 21-12-18		Company employed as above.	Nil

A5834 Wt. W4973/M687 750,000 8/16 D.D.&L. Ltd. Forms/C.2118/13.

Army Form C. 2118.

WAR DIARY

INTELLIGENCE SUMMARY.

(Erase heading not required.)

Ref. Map. NAMUR. 1:100,000.

Place	Date	Hour	Summary of Events and Information	Remarks and references to Appendices
CHARLEROI	22-12-18		Church Parade in morning and Commencement of filling up of demobilisation forms. Holiday for rest of day except for men specially employed on evans.	AHW.
	23-12-18 to 24-12-18		Work on coatlimbers, latrines etc for DHQ. Came for 127 Bde TRA continued, also improvements on Company Transport Lines. It was decided to try and put into working order a permanent bath found in CHARLEROI and by heating to make the water suitable for use in winter. Suitable vertical boilers were created and required stores collected.	AHW.
	25-12-18 26-12-18		Two days holiday. Special dinners arranged on Xmas day followed by dances, concert & whist drives on both days.	AHW.
	27-12-18 to 31-12-18		Work for RA continued and the wiring in of an Army Ration Dump at MONTIGNIES begun. Two vertical boilers transported from a factory to swimming baths and one temporarily fixed. Circulation water pipes of wood made ready for fixing. Steel for DHQ latrines commenced and 1 Section detailed to work under 429 Field Co on large Demobilisation camp at JUMET. Work at FLEURUS for 127 Bde continues & improvements to baths in Colliery there begun.	AHW AHW AHW AHW
			Casualties. Major J. Entwistle proceeds on month's leave Capt. A.N. Walker returns from leave. Lieut. H.C. Whitehead joined for duty from the Base.	AHW AHW AHW

A.N.Walker Capt. RE.
Commanding 428 Field Co RE.

WO 24
42

War Diary
of
428th (E. Lancs) Field Coy RE
from Jan. 1st to 31st 1919.

(Volume 6)

ORIGINAL
Conf Journal

Army Form C. 2118.

WAR DIARY
INTELLIGENCE SUMMARY.
(Erase heading not required.)

Ref. Maps.
BELGIUM. NAMUR Sheet 8. 1:100,000

Place	Date	Hour	Summary of Events and Information	Remarks and references to Appendices
CHARLEROI.	1-1-19 to 7-1-19		Company billeted at JESUIT COLLEGE, CHARLEROI, with transport lines at DAMPREMY. Coy employed on making a large factory at JUMET suitable for a demobilisation Concentration Camp (1 Section under orders of O.C. 449 Field Coy R.E.); on swimming baths in CHARLEROI where two vertical boilers were installed and connections made whereby steam was admitted to the bath and by means of a circulating pipe the temperature of the water was raised to an average of 70° Fahr; on completing minor services for D.H.Q.; on continuance of supplying water troughs, latrines, taken refuse for R.A. and on construction of mangers and general improvements on Coy transport lines Minor Services for 127 & Inty Bde at FLEURUS continued. 60.R. proceed to U.K. for demobilisation on 2-1-19.	/.
	8-1-19.		Billets of Monies Section at DAMPREMY broken into by persons unknown and a considerable quantity of Government property stolen. Workmen Concentration Camp at JUMET staffed and Sappers there released put on to construction of wire fence round a Ration Dump at MONTIGNIES.	/.
	9-1-19.		7 O.R. proceeded to U.K. for demobilisation.	/.
	10-1-19 to 12-1-19		Work continued as above, with additional work on Divisional Theatre preparing scenery for forthcoming show by Divisional Party.	/.

Army Form C. 2118.

WAR DIARY
of
Ry Map.
INTELLIGENCE SUMMARY. BELGIUM. NAMUR. Sheet 8. 1/100,000.

(Erase heading not required.)

Instructions regarding War Diaries and Intelligence Summaries are contained in F. S. Regs., Part II. and the Staff Manual respectively. Title pages will be prepared in manuscript.

Place	Date	Hour	Summary of Events and Information	Remarks and references to Appendices
CHARLEROI.	13-1-19.		All Coy. Section except No. 2 now withdrawn from FLEURUS front, work with 127th Inf. Bde.	/E.
	14-1-19.		Lieut. J. TATHER, R.E. transferred from 428 Field Coy to 407 Field Coy.	/E.
	15-1-19.		Work continued as above with additional task of constructing unloading stage for barges at CHATELINEAU.	/E.
			5 O.R. proceeded to U.K. for demobilisation.	
	16-1-19. to 17-1-19.		Unloading stage completed and checking of Company equipment commenced.	/E.
	18-1-19.		Party of 1 Officer and 23 O.R. detailed to attend Divisional presentation of medal Ribbons. Recipients from Coy. Major J. ENTWISTLE, M.C. and Capt. J.M. SCOTT. Croix de Guerre (French).	/E.
	19-1-19. to 26-1-19.		Coy. employed at above work assisted by working parties from 17 N.F. (Pioneers). Following were proceeded to U.K. for demobilisation. 10. O.R on 19.1.19. 3. O.R on 20.1.19. 1 O.R on 21.1.19. 8 O.R on 22.1.19. 1 O.R on 26.1.19.	/E.
	27-1-19.		Boxing ring erected at UNIVERSITE du TRAVAIL Charleroi, used as Brie. Theatre completed. 13 O.R. proceeded to U.K. for demobilisation.	/E.

Army Form C. 2118.

WAR DIARY
or
INTELLIGENCE SUMMARY.
(Erase heading not required.)

Ryhark.
BELGIUM. NAMUR. Sheet 8. 1:100,000

Place	Date	Hour	Summary of Events and Information	Remarks and references to Appendices
CHARLEROI	28-1-19 to 31-1-19		Owing to reduced Number Company employed on decreasing amount of work. With assistance of Civilian labour 2 German huts partially erected for RA at Montignies; Boxing ring dismantled & stored in RE Dump for future use. Minor repairs at Cr Hqrs, Cr Transport lines & Rest Theatre carried out.	R.
			Total OR demobilised during month = 49. " " released whilst on leave = 5.	R.
			Casualties.	
	9-1-19 24-1-19		Major J. ENTWISTLE M.C. rejoined Cy from leave in UK. Lieut L.J. MARR - to leave in UK.	R.
			Strength. Effective 7 Officers 188 OR. 6 Officers 154 OR. Ration 6 Officers 147 OR. 5 Officers 104 OR.	R.
	1-1-19 31-1-19			

[signature]
Major
Commdg 478 Field Cy RE.

WR26 W ORIGINAL
Army Form C. 2118.

WAR DIARY

INTELLIGENCE SUMMARY

(Erase heading not required.)

Instructions regarding War Diaries and Intelligence Summaries are contained in F.S. Regs., Part II. and the Staff Manual respectively. Title pages will be prepared in manuscript.

428th (East Lancs) Field Coy. R.E.

FEBRUARY 1919.

Place	Date	Hour	Summary of Events and Information	Remarks and references to Appendices
CHARLEROI.	1-2-19		Company Headquarters and dismounted portion of Company situated in BOULEVARD AUDENT; mounted section & Transport lines on the RUE DE BRUXELLES. 25 German P.O.W. arrived for work on Transport lines - assisting generally. 19 O.R. despatched to IV Corps Concentration Camp for release. Small part of Sunday was taken up. Kit inspection carried out during morning.	
	2.2.19		Engaged on work & fire precautions at Divisional Theatre.	
	3.2.19		Work continued - 1 O.R. sent to Kents lines to work for 3 hrs. first time were returned. Out 2 huts to be erected for R.F.A. and hence stores for A.	
	4th 2.19 to		G.R.E. Dump. Erecting Boxing Ring on the Manoeuvre outdoor with judges platform etc.; afternoons dismantled and places at R.E. Dump. Completes the erection of 2 huts for C.211 Battery R.F.A. on the MONTIGNIES - GILLY Road. Supervision of making of tables forms. All surplus stores returned to G.R.E. Dump. Work of section disinfector for 127 by 52e. at REVERS, tied up owing to severe weather. Commence erection of 60' x 20' Canteen hut for IV Corps Concert Camp.	
	12.2.19		At MARCHIENNE, and 2 small marquees for D.A.D.R.T. at CHARLEROI manufacture. The Caller M 757. Complete a wooden floor, working on estimating contents of abandoned enemy cable dump in C DADO.S completed. All Company, bicycles, watches, prismatic compasses handed in to DADO.S. on 5th inst.	
	7.2.19		13 O.R. and 6/2/19 ┐ despatched to U.K. for release. Capt A.H. WALKER & 3 O.R. on 9/2/19 ┘ 1 O.R. Lieut. PETRY proceeded on 8 days leave to PARIS.	

A. 1092. W. W2839/M1293. 750,000. 1/17. D.D. & L. Ltd. Forms/C2118/14.

WAR DIARY
or
INTELLIGENCE SUMMARY.

Army Form C. 2118.

Place	Date	Hour	Summary of Events and Information	Remarks and references to Appendices
CHARLEROI	13/2/19 to 18/2/19.		Being rung again at Université du Travail CHARLEROI, erk sledge platforms etc. and afterwards dismantled and all stores turned over to Australian Infantry. Repairing floor in Stables occupied by the Company's animals at DAMPREMY. Work on canteen hut at MARCHIENNE and erection of 2 french marquees at train Station, CHARLEROI carried on with. 5 OR on 14/2/19 } dispatched to 'CONCENT' (IV Corps Concentration Camp) 1 OR on 15/2/19 } for demobilization. 2/Lt LORD proceeded to 'CONCENT' as Staff Conducting Officer 18.2.19. 2/Lt PETRY rejoined Coy. from leave in PARIS on 16.2.19 A further 15 (P.O.W) (making 37 in all) attached to Div R.E. for work Checking 1 Comp Stores going on daily. 9 L.D. 1 (Y) horses dispatched to HAVRE, entraining at CHARLEROI Station	
	19.2.19.		at 0900 hrs on 18.2.19. A fire broke out at D.H.Q. (Top storey) at 1800 hrs, and a portion of the roof was completely gutted. All available troops were gathered together and were with a chain with which buckets of water were passed quickly along, and with the assistance of the 'Charleroi fire Brigade', the fire was subdued about 2000 hrs. During the repair horses tolling the Company waterload was damaged) and was sent to the R.E. Ordnance workshops for repair. 6 O.R. were despatched to 'CONCENT' for release.	

Army Form C. 2118.

WAR DIARY
or
INTELLIGENCE SUMMARY
(Erase heading not required)

Instructions regarding War Diaries and Intelligence Summaries are contained in F.S. Regs., Part II. and the Staff Manual respectively. Title pages will be prepared in manuscript.

426

Place	Date	Hour	Summary of Events and Information	Remarks and references to Appendices
CHARLEROI	20/2/19		Preparing plan re D.H.Q. prior Commences work at ONOZ – 6 platforms for S.A.A. Gun Amm.	
	21/2/19.		Pleasant rest for Divisional Vehicle Park. Comp. reduced to Cadre 'B' strength. Still 26 o.R. on leave when circumstances will not permit. Runners & Kits unit.	
			1 L.D. (T Class) horse despatches ETAIRE work at CHARLEROI Station almost complete. Checking stores and preparing to put men in Infantry Barracks at Charleroi.	
	22/2/19.		work carried on at ONOZ and D.H.Q. and at MARCHIENNE.	
	23/2/19. to 28/2/19.		B.O.R. proceeding to 'CEMENT' for demobilization. Work at CHARLEROI Station & Canteen hut completed. Provision of 10 seats Latrine with arches and absent complete. 2 hand magnets erected complete with wooden floors & stoves. Alterations to partitions when the main Canteen / Drying station. Cookers to doors, provision of rifle racks – further work re Canteen will be carried out by German P.O.W.s. Coy Equipment complete as checked with G.1098 Stores placed in CHARLEROI Infantry Barracks. Coy. vehicles parked in Div Vehicle Park. and receipts obtained. Instructions received for all units to be prepared to drop to Cadre 'A' at short notice – all papers & particulars of Cadre 'B' (m.g.) now being prepared at once and necessary Army Forms for these men	

Army Form C. 2118.

WAR DIARY
or
INTELLIGENCE SUMMARY

(Erase heading not required.)

Instructions regarding War Diaries and Intelligence Summaries are contained in F. S. Regs., Part II. and the Staff Manual respectively. Title pages will be prepared in manuscript.

Place	Date	Hour	Summary of Events and Information	Remarks and references to Appendices
CHARLEROI	23/2/19.		alignment ready.	
			9 Riding horses } 'Z' } Sold to Belgian Civilians 25/2/19.	G.
			4 L.D. } Class	
	28/2/19. (continued)		4 L.D. } mules } Class	
			1 Pack }	
			4 Riding horses } Z Class	do
			1 L.D. }	
			9 L.D. } mules	
			1 Pack }	
			2 L.D. horses ('X' class) stolen during night 23/24 inst. from Compy. Stables	27/2/19. G.
			at Transport Lines.	
			1 L.D. (Y horse) despatched to HAVRE 27/2/19.	
			Strength of Coy.	
			1/2/19: 6 officers 154 O.R.	
			28/2/19: 5 officers 98 O.R. - two instances 17 O.R. who have probably been demobilized whilst on leave (having sailed before 10/11/19) but for whom no official notification has been received	G.

428TH
(EAST LANCS.)
FIELD COMPANY, R.E.
No. ....
Date 28/2/19

[signature]
Major
O.C. 428th Fd. Coy. R.E.

Army Form C. 2118.

WAR DIARY
INTELLIGENCE SUMMARY
(Erase heading not required.)

428th (East Lancs.) Field Coy. R.E.

MARCH 1919.

Place	Date	Hour	Summary of Events and Information	Remarks and references to Appendices
CHARLEROI.	1st	—	Company reduced to Cadre B strength - plus 15 O.R. on leave in U.K. but awaiting demobilysis whilst on leave. Cadre situated at JESUIT COLLEGE, Boulevard Audent.	
			CHARLEROI: Clone in hand:— All explosives in possession of Company being moved to ONOZ ammunition dump. Odd jobs carried out at Charleroi Main Station for D.A.D.R.T. All box respirators of released officers & O.R. withdrawn and returned to D.A.D.O.S.	
	2nd		Ammn. 1 S.R.	
	3rd to 5th		Great show lost exertion on night 2/3 ult. It was recovered by DEPOT M. 37 Divn. from Belgian Police. A further 4 "Z" animals were disposed of to the Belgian Civilians including the "Atom" recovered, leaves a total of 128 animals now remaining with the unit. 35 German P.O.W. joined Company.	
	6th		Sraz Barnes (1 Sect. Company) and 1 R.S. wagon with equipment from 42 Div Train. A little work in Charleroi Station, then engaged repacking of stores, harness, etc. into crates at default Barracks.	
	7th		Lt Ham taken command during temporary absence of O.C. Lieut. WHITEHEAD and 1 O.R. demobilized, Proceed to IV Corps Concentration Camp. One "Z" pack horse sold in Charleroi - 27 animals now remain with Company.	
	8th to 20th		Packing of Company equipment etc. Rationing same in default Barracks, proceeded with loose packages. Name of Company painted on all vehicles and loose packages.	

WAR DIARY
INTELLIGENCE SUMMARY.

Army Form C. 2118.

Place	Date	Hour	Summary of Events and Information	Remarks and references to Appendices
CHARLEROI	8th to 20th (Continued)		54 P.O.W. handed over to G.R.A. at MONTIGNY on 10/3/19. Lt LORD rejoined Company from leave in U.K. 11/3/19 - Major ENTWISTLE to short leave in U.K. on 12/3/19 - rejoined Coy on 18.3.19. 3 O.R. returned to U.K. for release, 3 O.R. despatched to U.K. for release 15/3/19. Lt PETRY to leave in U.K. 16/3/19. Lt MAPER proceeded to 427 Fd. Cy R.E. 20/3/19. Lt TAYLER posted to this unit. 1 O.R. joined Company from R.F.B.D. 18/3/19. 1 R. I.K.D. horses despatched to HAVRE 18/3/19. 3 R.Q.L.D. handed over to R.F.A.G.C. 20/3/19.	OK. OK.
	21st to 28th		A further 6 animals (Shorter Animals) despatched to HAVRE on 23/3/19. 7 animals not remain with unit. None of destination (OSWESTRY) painted on all vehicles - book sides - and all loose packages etc. not in vehicles. 2 O.R. despatched to CONCENT for release. 5 O.R. (plus 1 on leave) despatched to Eastern Division COLOGNE on 27.3.19. Sgt. ERGE and 1 O.R. (including 1 on leave) transferred to 1st Army R.E. 22/3/19. 4 O.R. returned new who proceeded on 14 days leave in U.K. before 12/1/19 now struck 8 O.R. returnable new on instructions from Division. Unit now reduced to (adn. + plus 67% (27r) + to all for sick wastage, and plus 2 officers (1 for A.D.O. and 1 for repatriation) : (home Strength, 4 officers 53 O.R.) 1 3 O.R. returned to 42 Bn. P.O.W. Companies on 22/3/19. 3 Riding horses handed over to R.G.A. 3 A.D. mules handed to this unit from 429 Fd. Cy. R.E. } which still leave remain with the unit.	OK. OK. OK. OK. OK. OK.

WAR DIARY
or
INTELLIGENCE SUMMARY.
(Erase heading not required.)

Army Form C. 2118.

Place	Date	Hour	Summary of Events and Information	Remarks and references to Appendices
CHAPELLE ST	29th to 31st		All preparations being made for the forthcoming move to ANTWERP (by train) commencing on 2nd April. 2 W.D. horses (one being an "S.S." horse) despatched to Base (OUTREAU) on 31/3/19. — his leaves us 5 W.D. mules in possession of Coy. — these latter have been handed over to 457 Fd Coy. R.E. leaving this unit with no animals at all.	

[signature]
Major
O.C. 428th Fd. Coy. R.E.

428TH
(EAST LANCS.)
FIELD COMPANY, R.E.
No.
Date 31. 3. 19.

www.ingramcontent.com/pod-product-compliance
Lightning Source LLC
Chambersburg PA
CBHW081547160426
43191CB00011B/1862